WEEKDAYS

ARE

QUICK MEALS

from Speedy Stir-Fries to Soups to

Skillet Dishes and Thirty-Minute Stews

◆　　◆　　◆

TIME
LIFE®
BOOKS

TIME-LIFE BOOKS, ALEXANDRIA, VIRGINIA

TIME-LIFE BOOKS IS A DIVISION OF TIME LIFE INC.

TIME-LIFE CUSTOM PUBLISHING

Vice President and Publisher	Terry Newell
Project Manager	Jennifer Pearce
Director of Sales	Neil Levin
Director of New Product Development	Regina Hall
Managing Editor	Donia Ann Steele
Production Manager	Carolyn Mills Bounds
Quality Assurance Manager	Miriam P. Newton

PRODUCED BY ROUNDTABLE PRESS, INC.

Directors	Marsha Melnick, Susan E. Meyer
Senior Editor	Carol Spier
Text and Recipe Development	Kathy Farrell-Kingsley
Assistant Editor	Abigail Anderson
Production	Steven Rosen

ILLUSTRATIONS
William Neeper

Library of Congress Cataloging-in-Publication Data
Weekdays are quick meals : from speedy stir-fries to soups to skillet
dishes and thirty-minute stews / the editors of Time-Life Books.
        p.   cm.
    Includes index.
    ISBN 0-7835-4834-6
        1. Quick and easy cookery.   2. Dinners and dining   I. Time-Life
    Books.
    TX833.5.W44   1996
    641.5′55--dc20   96-7946
                                                                CIP

Books produced by Time-Life Custom Publishing are available
at special bulk discount for promotional and premium use.
Custom adaptations can also be created to meet
your specific marketing goals.
Call 1-800-323-5255.

Introduction

"I don't have time to cook." You know the feeling. But *Weekdays Are Quick Meals* will make your kitchen work faster. Tonight, in the time it would take to purchase dinner at a deli or restaurant, you can put a delicious homemade meal on your table. All the recipes in this book can be made in 30 minutes or less—from cupboard to table—and many are based on family-friendly yields of four servings. Speed your way to the best entrées ever, like Maple-Glazed Lamb Chops or Sweet and Sour Chicken Stir-Fry. It's also simple to add a touch of elegance to your entrées with some tasty accompaniments such as Herbed Rice Pilaf or Wild Mushroom Stir-Fry. So no matter what your needs are, from easy elegance for unexpected dinner guests to a meal on-the-run before dashing off to a ball game, you'll be prepared.

This cookbook also offers a variety of shortcuts and tips for weekday cooking. For example, all recipes have few ingredients and use fast-cooking techniques such as grilling, broiling, and stir-frying. The result is sumptuous yet simple meals that are ready in minutes. And to further conserve your time, the ingredients called for are readily available in the supermarket or pantry. Throughout the book helpful notes offer speedy dessert ideas, simple variations to the recipes, ingredient substitutions, and helpful kitchen tips.

As an additional bonus, many of these recipes get fewer than 30 percent of their calories from fat! These recipes are labeled "Low-Fat" and are marked with this symbol: ♡ (A full listing of the low-fat recipes is included in the index under the heading "Low-Fat.")

So, the next time you're about to say, "I don't have time to cook," reach for *Weekdays Are Quick Meals* instead. You'll be happy you did!

—*Mara Reid Rogers,*
author of numerous cookbooks and
spokesperson for The Everyday Cookbooks

Contents

Skillet Dishes and Stir-Fries

Accompaniments

Index

SOUPS AND STEWS

POTATO LEEK SOUP

SERVES 4

1 TABLESPOON UNSALTED BUTTER

1 GARLIC CLOVE, MINCED

2 LEEKS, TRIMMED, HALVED LENGTHWISE, RINSED WELL, AND CHOPPED

ONE 16-OUNCE CAN POTATOES, DRAINED

3½ CUPS CHICKEN BROTH, PREFERABLY REDUCED-SODIUM

¼ TEASPOON SALT

¼ TEASPOON BLACK PEPPER

½ CUP HALF-AND-HALF

1. In a large saucepan, warm the butter over medium heat until melted. Add the garlic and leeks and sauté until the leeks are softened, about 5 minutes.

2. Add the potatoes, chicken broth, salt, and pepper, and bring the mixture to a boil over medium-high heat. Reduce the heat to medium-low, cover, and simmer for 5 minutes.

3. Purée the soup in batches in a food processor. Return the soup to the saucepan and stir in the half-and-half. Warm the soup over low heat.

KITCHEN NOTE: *Leeks need to be thoroughly cleaned before using to remove all the dirt trapped between the leaf layers. This is easily done by first trimming the green leafy ends so that about 5 inches remain. Then slit the leek from the top to the bottom and rinse under cold running water.*

Sweet Corn and Ham Chowder

SERVES 4

2 TABLESPOONS UNSALTED BUTTER
1 LARGE ONION, FINELY CHOPPED
1 TEASPOON DRY MUSTARD
3 CUPS FROZEN CORN KERNELS,
    THAWED
3 CUPS MILK OR HALF-AND-HALF

ONE 15-OUNCE CAN SMALL WHITE
    POTATOES, DRAINED AND DICED
1 CUP DICED HAM
¼ TEASPOON SALT
¼ TEASPOON BLACK PEPPER

1. In a large saucepan, warm the butter over medium heat until melted. Add the onion and sauté until softened, about 5 minutes. Stir in the mustard.

2. Meanwhile, in a food processor or a blender, purée 1 cup of the corn with 1 cup of the milk. Add the purée to the pan.

3. Stir in the remaining corn, the remaining milk, the potatoes, ham, salt, and pepper. Cook over medium-low heat, stirring often, until corn is tender and soup is heated through, about 10 minutes. (Do not let the soup boil.)

Kitchen Note: *It is widely believed that the word chowder derives from the French word "chaudière," a large cauldron that French sailors and fishermen put their catch into for a communal stew.*

Cream of Broccoli and Cheddar Soup

SERVES 4

4 TABLESPOONS UNSALTED BUTTER
1 MEDIUM ONION, FINELY CHOPPED
3 TABLESPOONS FLOUR
1¾ CUPS CHICKEN BROTH, PREFERABLY
    REDUCED-SODIUM
ONE 10-OUNCE PACKAGE FROZEN
    CHOPPED BROCCOLI, THAWED AND
    DRAINED

8 OUNCES MILD CHEDDAR CHEESE,
    SHREDDED (2 CUPS)
1½ CUPS HALF-AND-HALF
½ TEASPOON SALT
¼ TEASPOON BLACK PEPPER

1. In a large saucepan, warm the butter over medium heat until melted. Add the onion and sauté until softened, about 5 minutes. Stir in the flour and cook over low heat, stirring constantly, until no longer visible, about 1 minute.

2. Slowly stir in the broth, then the broccoli. Bring the mixture to a boil over medium-high heat. Reduce the heat to medium-low, cover, and simmer until the broccoli is tender, about 10 minutes.

3. Stir in the Cheddar cheese and cook over low heat until melted, about 30 seconds. Stir in the half-and-half, salt, and pepper. Warm the soup over low heat. (Do not let the soup boil.)

KITCHEN NOTE: *Here's a handy time-saving tip: One 13¾-ounce can of chicken broth contains 1¾ cups, so there is no need to measure when that's the amount the recipe calls for.*

Chicken and Mushroom Soup

 LOW-FAT

3 TABLESPOONS UNSALTED BUTTER

1 MEDIUM ONION, FINELY CHOPPED

2½ CUPS THINLY SLICED MUSHROOMS

1 TABLESPOON TOMATO PASTE

3½ CUPS CHICKEN BROTH, PREFERABLY
    REDUCED-SODIUM

1 POUND SKINLESS, BONELESS CHICKEN
    BREAST HALVES

2 CUPS THIN EGG NOODLES

½ TEASPOON SALT

½ TEASPOON BLACK PEPPER

¼ CUP CHOPPED FRESH PARSLEY

1. In a large saucepan, warm the butter over medium heat until melted. Add the onion and sauté until softened, about 5 minutes. Add the mushrooms and sauté until softened, about 5 minutes.

2. Stir in the tomato paste, chicken broth, and 1 cup water, and bring to a boil over medium-high heat.

3. Meanwhile, cut the chicken on the diagonal into ½-inch-wide strips. Add to the pan with the noodles, salt, and pepper.

4. Reduce the heat to medium-low, cover, and simmer for about 8 minutes, stirring occasionally, until the chicken is cooked through and the noodles are tender. Stir in the parsley.

Tomato Vegetable Soup with Pesto

SERVES 4

1 TABLESPOON OLIVE OIL

1 LARGE ONION, CHOPPED

1 MEDIUM ZUCCHINI, CUT IN HALF
LENGTHWISE, THEN SLICED

1 MEDIUM YELLOW SQUASH, CUT IN
HALF LENGTHWISE, THEN SLICED

1 GARLIC CLOVE, MINCED

3½ CUPS CHICKEN BROTH, PREFERABLY
REDUCED SODIUM

ONE 16-OUNCE CAN WHOLE TOMATOES
IN JUICE, DRAINED AND CHOPPED

ONE 15-OUNCE CAN WHITE KIDNEY
BEANS, RINSED AND DRAINED

2 TABLESPOONS READY-MADE PESTO

GRATED ROMANO CHEESE FOR GARNISH
(OPTIONAL)

1. In a large saucepan, warm the oil over medium heat. Add the onion and sauté until softened, about 5 minutes. Add the zucchini, yellow squash, and garlic and sauté until the squash is crisp-tender, about 5 minutes.

2. Stir in the chicken broth, tomatoes, beans, and pesto. Simmer, uncovered, over medium heat for 10 minutes.

3. Ladle into soup bowls and sprinkle with the grated Romano cheese, if desired.

KITCHEN NOTE: *Ready-made pesto is available in most large supermarkets, either refrigerated or in jars. But if you have access to fresh basil, you may want to make it from scratch. Here's one recipe: In a food processor or blender, purée 1 cup packed basil leaves, ½ cup flat-leaf parsley, ⅓ cup olive oil, ¼ cup walnuts, ¼ cup chicken broth, 1 garlic clove, ½ teaspoon salt, and ¼ teaspoon black pepper. Scrape into an airtight container and refrigerate.*

Tortellini and Spinach Soup

SERVES 4

6 CUPS REDUCED-SODIUM CHICKEN
  BROTH
¾ POUND FRESH OR FROZEN CHEESE
  TORTELLINI
2 CUPS COARSELY CHOPPED FRESH
  SPINACH LEAVES

⅛ TEASPOON BLACK PEPPER
2 TABLESPOONS GRATED PARMESAN
  CHEESE

1. In a large saucepan, bring the chicken broth to a boil over medium-high heat. Add the tortellini and cook until tender, 10 to 12 minutes for fresh, 15 minutes for frozen.

2. Reduce the heat to medium-low. Stir in the spinach and simmer, uncovered, until wilted, about 2 minutes. Season with the pepper.

3. Ladle into soup bowls and sprinkle with Parmesan cheese.

SWEET AFTERTHOUGHT: *To satisfy a craving for something sweet after a meal, try this super-quick and light dessert. Melt some seedless raspberry jam and pour it over lemon sherbet, then top with toasted coconut.*

Asian Shrimp-Noodle Soup

SERVES 4

♡ LOW-FAT

6 CUPS REDUCED-SODIUM CHICKEN
   BROTH
4 CUPS SHREDDED GREEN CABBAGE
1 GARLIC CLOVE, MINCED
1 TEASPOON MINCED FRESH GINGER
2½ CUPS SNOW PEAS, CUT IN HALF
   CROSSWISE

6 OUNCES CAPELLINI, BROKEN INTO
   THIRDS (2 CUPS)
3 TABLESPOONS TERIYAKI SAUCE
1½ POUNDS PEELED, COOKED SMALL
   SHRIMP
2 TABLESPOONS ORIENTAL (DARK)
   SESAME OIL

1. In a large saucepan, bring the chicken broth and 3 cups water to a boil over medium-high heat. Stir in the cabbage, garlic, and ginger and boil gently over medium heat for 4 to 5 minutes.

2. Stir in the snow peas, capellini, and teriyaki sauce and boil gently until the cabbage and pasta are tender, about 3 minutes.

3. Stir in the shrimp and sesame oil and serve.

KITCHEN NOTE: *Dark sesame oil is pressed from sesame seeds and has a nutty flavor and fragrance. It is almost always used as a flavoring rather than for cooking, because heat will alter its taste. A light-colored, cold-pressed sesame oil is also available, but it has a milder flavor and is not a good substitute for the dark variety.*

HEARTY BEEF AND VEGETABLE SOUP

SERVES 4

2 TABLESPOONS VEGETABLE OIL
1 MEDIUM ONION, FINELY CHOPPED
1 GARLIC CLOVE, MINCED
6 CUPS REDUCED-SODIUM BEEF BROTH
ONE 16-OUNCE BAG MIXED
    VEGETABLES, SUCH AS PEAS,
    CARROTS, AND CAULIFLOWER

1 CUP DITALINI OR OTHER SMALL
    TUBULAR PASTA
½ POUND BEEF ROUND STIR-FRY
    STRIPS, CUT IN HALF CROSSWISE

1. In a large saucepan, warm 1 tablespoon of the oil over medium-high heat. Add the onion and garlic and sauté until the onion is softened, about 3 minutes. Add the beef broth and bring to a boil over high heat.

2. Stir in the vegetables and pasta and return the soup to a boil. Reduce the heat to medium and boil gently until the pasta and vegetables are tender, about 8 minutes.

3. Meanwhile, in a large skillet, warm the remaining tablespoon of oil over medium-high heat. Add the beef strips and stir-fry until browned, about 5 minutes.

4. Divide the beef among 4 soup bowls. Ladle the hot soup over the beef and serve.

Pasta e Fagioli

SERVES 4

2 TABLESPOONS OLIVE OIL
2 GARLIC CLOVES, MINCED
ONE 16-OUNCE CAN PEELED PLUM
   TOMATOES, DRAINED
½ TEASPOON DRIED OREGANO

ONE 16-OUNCE CAN CANNELLINI
   BEANS, RINSED AND DRAINED
1 CUP DITALINI OR ELBOW MACARONI
¼ TEASPOON SALT

1. In a large saucepan, warm the oil over medium heat. Add the garlic and sauté for 30 seconds. Add the tomatoes and oregano and break up the tomatoes with the back of a large spoon.

2. Stir in the beans and 3½ cups water and bring the mixture to a boil over medium-high heat. Reduce the heat to medium-low and simmer, uncovered, for 10 minutes.

3. Purée half of the soup in a food processor. Return the purée to the pan and return the soup to a boil over medium-high heat.

4. Add the pasta. Reduce the heat to medium-low and simmer, uncovered, until the pasta is tender, about 10 minutes. Season with the salt.

KITCHEN NOTE: *Because pasta and beans combine to form a complete protein, this recipe is not only tasty—it's good for you.*

Santa Fe Chicken Stew

SERVES 4

1 TABLESPOON VEGETABLE OIL
1½ POUNDS SKINLESS, BONELESS
  CHICKEN THIGHS
1 MEDIUM ONION, THINLY SLICED
2 GARLIC CLOVES, MINCED
2 TABLESPOONS CHILI POWDER
ONE 14½-OUNCE CAN STEWED
  TOMATOES

ONE 15-OUNCE CAN BLACK BEANS OR
  PINTO BEANS, RINSED AND DRAINED
⅓ CUP CHOPPED FRESH CILANTRO
½ TEASPOON SALT
½ TEASPOON BLACK PEPPER

1. In a large skillet, warm the oil over medium-high heat. Add the chicken and sauté until browned, about 6 minutes.

2. Reduce the heat to medium, stir in the onion, garlic, and chili powder, and cook, stirring frequently, until the onion is softened, about 3 minutes.

3. Add the tomatoes and beans. Simmer, stirring occasionally, until chicken is cooked through and juices have thickened, about 10 minutes. Stir in the cilantro and season with the salt and pepper.

Variation: *Dress up this spicy chicken stew with your choice of the following garnishes: sour cream, black olives, grated Monterey Jack cheese, chopped jalapeño peppers, tomato, green bell pepper, or scallions.*

30-Minute Chili

SERVES 4

½ POUND LEAN GROUND BEEF
1 TABLESPOON CHILI POWDER
1 TEASPOON GROUND CUMIN
1 MEDIUM ONION, CHOPPED
1 MEDIUM GREEN BELL PEPPER,
  CHOPPED
2 GARLIC CLOVES, MINCED

ONE 15-OUNCE CAN SMALL RED
  KIDNEY BEANS, RINSED AND
  DRAINED
1 CUP BOTTLED SPAGHETTI SAUCE
CHOPPED SCALLIONS, SOUR CREAM,
  AND SHREDDED MONTEREY JACK
  CHEESE, FOR GARNISH (OPTIONAL)

1. In a large nonstick skillet, cook the beef, stirring frequently, until browned, about 5 minutes. Stir in the chili powder and cumin.

2. Add the onion, bell pepper, and garlic, and cook, stirring frequently, until the onion is softened, about 3 minutes.

3. Stir in the beans and spaghetti sauce. Cover and simmer over medium-low heat until heated through, about 5 minutes.

4. Serve the chili with bowls of scallions, sour cream, and shredded Monterey Jack cheese on the side, if desired.

VARIATION: *This chili can also be easily made into a vegetarian version. Just omit the ground beef, add the spices to the onion mixture, and add another 15-ounce can of rinsed and drained kidney beans or a different kind, such as pink, white, or black beans.*

Island Seafood Stew

SERVES 4

2 TABLESPOONS VEGETABLE OIL

1 LARGE ONION, CHOPPED

1 LARGE YELLOW BELL PEPPER, CHOPPED

2 GARLIC CLOVES, MINCED

2 TEASPOONS CURRY POWDER

⅓ CUP CANNED CREAM OF COCONUT

⅓ CUP BOTTLED CLAM JUICE

ONE 28-OUNCE CAN PEELED PLUM TOMATOES, DRAINED AND CHOPPED

¼ CUP FRESH LIME JUICE

1 POUND FIRM WHITE FISH FILLETS, SUCH AS COD, RED SNAPPER, OR MONKFISH, CUT INTO 2-INCH PIECES

2 TABLESPOONS CHOPPED FRESH CILANTRO

½ TEASPOON SALT

1. In a large saucepan, warm the oil over medium heat. Add the onion and bell pepper and sauté until softened, about 5 minutes. Add the garlic and curry powder and cook for 1 minute.

2. Stir in the cream of coconut, clam juice, and tomatoes, and bring to a boil over medium-high heat. Reduce the heat to medium-low and simmer, partially covered, for 10 minutes.

3. Stir in the lime juice. Add the fish and simmer, uncovered, over low heat just until cooked through, 2 to 3 minutes. Stir in the cilantro and simmer for 1 minute. Season with the salt.

SWEET AFTERTHOUGHT: *Complete this tropical dinner with a dessert of fresh cut-up ripe mango topped with ginger whipped cream. To make the ginger whipped cream: In a medium bowl, combine 1 cup heavy cream, 3 tablespoons confectioners' sugar, and 1 teaspoon ground ginger. Beat with an electric mixer until soft peaks form.*

Southern Sausage Stew

SERVES 4

1 TABLESPOON VEGETABLE OIL
½ POUND FULLY COOKED SMOKED
    SAUSAGE, SUCH AS ANDOUILLE OR
    KIELBASA, CUT INTO ¼-INCH-THICK
    SLICES
TWO 14½-OUNCE CANS STEWED
    TOMATOES
ONE 10-OUNCE PACKAGE FROZEN LIMA
    BEANS, THAWED

ONE 11-OUNCE CAN VACUUM-PACKED
    CORN KERNELS
½ TEASPOON GARLIC POWDER
½ TEASPOON PAPRIKA
¼ TEASPOON DRIED OREGANO
¼ TEASPOON CAYENNE PEPPER
¼ TEASPOON BLACK PEPPER

1. In a large saucepan, warm the oil over medium-high heat. Add the sausage and cook, stirring frequently, until browned, about 5 minutes.

2. Add the tomatoes, beans, corn, garlic powder, paprika, oregano, cayenne, and black pepper. Cook over medium heat, stirring occasionally, until the beans are cooked through and the mixture has thickened slightly, about 15 minutes.

MAIN COURSE SALADS

WARM BEEF AND SPINACH SALAD

SERVES 4

ONE 10-OUNCE BAG FRESH SPINACH,
STEMMED AND TORN INTO BITE-SIZE
PIECES

¾ POUND THINLY SLICED RARE ROAST
BEEF, CUT CROSSWISE INTO THIN
STRIPS

6 TABLESPOONS OLIVE OIL

2 MEDIUM RED BELL PEPPERS, CUT
INTO THIN STRIPS

1 SMALL ONION, THINLY SLICED

1 GARLIC CLOVE, MINCED

3 TABLESPOONS BALSAMIC VINEGAR

2 TEASPOONS DIJON MUSTARD

½ TEASPOON SALT

½ TEASPOON BLACK PEPPER

1. In a large serving bowl, combine the spinach and roast beef. Set aside.

2. In a large skillet, warm 2 tablespoons of the oil over medium-high heat. Add the bell peppers, onion, and garlic and sauté until the vegetables are softened, 2 to 3 minutes.

3. Add the remaining 4 tablespoons of oil, the vinegar, mustard, salt, and pepper to the skillet and cook, stirring often, until warmed through, 1 to 2 minutes. Pour the warm dressing over the spinach mixture and toss well to coat evenly. Serve warm.

KITCHEN NOTE: *Spinach leaves need to be thoroughly rinsed to remove any sand and grit. The best way to clean spinach is to put it in a large bowl of cold water, then change the water 2 or 3 times. To avoid pouring the sandy water back over the spinach, lift the spinach out of the bowl with your hands each time, instead of draining it in a colander.*

Beef and Asparagus Vinaigrette

SERVES 4

1 POUND FRESH ASPARAGUS, TRIMMED
    AND CUT INTO 1-INCH PIECES
2 MEDIUM CARROTS, PEELED AND
    THINLY SLICED
2 TABLESPOONS RED WINE VINEGAR
1 TABLESPOON CHOPPED FRESH
    TARRAGON, OR 1 TEASPOON DRIED
1 TEASPOON DIJON MUSTARD

¼ TEASPOON SALT
¼ TEASPOON BLACK PEPPER
⅓ CUP OLIVE OIL
8 CUPS LOOSELY PACKED TORN MIXED
    GREENS, WASHED AND SPUN DRY
ONE 1-POUND PIECE OF RARE ROAST
    BEEF, CUT INTO THIN STRIPS

1. Bring a large saucepan of water to a boil over high heat. Add the asparagus and carrots and boil until crisp-tender, about 2 minutes. Drain the vegetables, rinse under cold running water, and drain well.

2. In a large bowl, whisk together the vinegar, tarragon, mustard, salt, and pepper. Slowly whisk in the oil until blended.

3. Add the greens to the dressing in the bowl and toss well to coat evenly. Add the asparagus, carrots, and beef, and toss well to combine the ingredients.

KITCHEN NOTE: *Always add vinaigrettes to salads containing asparagus, broccoli, or green beans at the last minute, which will help to keep the vegetables bright green.*

Sesame Beef Salad

SERVES 4

¾ POUND FLANK STEAK

1 MEDIUM CUCUMBER

1 PINT CHERRY TOMATOES

4 SCALLIONS

2 TABLESPOONS FRESH LIME JUICE

2 TABLESPOONS RICE WINE VINEGAR

¼ CUP CHOPPED FRESH MINT

1 TEASPOON MINCED FRESH GINGER

1 TEASPOON ORIENTAL (DARK) SESAME
OIL

⅓ CUP VEGETABLE OIL, PREFERABLY
PEANUT OIL

2 TABLESPOONS SESAME SEEDS,
TOASTED

1. Preheat the broiler. Line a broiler pan with foil.

2. Place the steak on the prepared broiler pan. Broil 4 inches from the heat for 5 to 6 minutes on each side for medium-rare meat.

3. Meanwhile, peel, seed, and chop the cucumber. Stem and halve the cherry tomatoes. Thinly slice the scallions. Set aside.

4. In a large bowl, whisk together the lime juice, vinegar, mint, ginger, and sesame oil. Slowly whisk in the oil until blended. Add the cucumber, tomatoes, and scallions to the bowl and toss well to coat.

5. Transfer the steak to a cutting board and let rest for 5 minutes. Thinly slice the steak across the grain and on the diagonal, add to the salad, and toss well to coat evenly. Sprinkle with the sesame seeds and serve.

KITCHEN NOTE: *Toasting seeds and nuts enhances their flavor. Toast sesame seeds in a small dry skillet over medium heat, stirring often, for 2 to 3 minutes, or until golden and fragrant.*

HAM AND BELL PEPPER COLESLAW

SERVES 4

1½ TABLESPOONS CIDER VINEGAR

1 TABLESPOON HONEY

1½ TEASPOONS BROWN SUGAR

½ TEASPOON CELERY SEED

¼ TEASPOON SALT

¼ CUP MAYONNAISE

ONE ¾-POUND PIECE OF HAM, CUT
INTO THIN STRIPS (3 CUPS)

1 MEDIUM RED BELL PEPPER, CUT INTO
THIN STRIPS

1 MEDIUM GREEN BELL PEPPER, CUT
INTO THIN STRIPS

1 MEDIUM YELLOW BELL PEPPER, CUT
INTO THIN STRIPS

¼ CUP CHOPPED FRESH PARSLEY

1. In a large bowl, whisk together the vinegar, honey, brown sugar, celery seed, and salt. Add the mayonnaise and whisk until blended.

2. Add the ham, bell peppers, and parsley to the bowl and toss well to combine and coat evenly with the dressing.

SUBSTITUTION: *This coleslaw can be made with almost any cooked meat such as roast beef, corned beef, chicken, or turkey.*

Italian Sausage and Couscous Salad

SERVES 6

1 CUP QUICK-COOKING COUSCOUS
¾ POUND HOT OR SWEET ITALIAN
    SAUSAGE, CASINGS REMOVED
2 MEDIUM RED BELL PEPPERS, DICED
3 SCALLIONS, THINLY SLICED
¾ CUP SLICED GREEN OLIVES WITH
    PIMIENTOS

3 TABLESPOONS WHITE WINE VINEGAR
2 GARLIC CLOVES, MINCED
1 TEASPOON DIJON MUSTARD
½ TEASPOON SALT
½ CUP OLIVE OIL

1. In a large heatproof serving bowl, combine the couscous and 1½ cups boiling water. Cover the bowl and let the couscous stand while you cook the sausage.

2. Crumble the sausage into a large nonstick skillet and cook over medium-high heat, stirring often, until browned, about 5 minutes. Drain the sausage on paper towels.

3. Fluff the couscous with a fork. Add the sausage, bell peppers, scallions, and olives to the couscous and toss well to combine.

4. In a small bowl, whisk together the vinegar, garlic, mustard, and salt. Slowly whisk in the oil until well blended. Pour the dressing over the salad and toss well to coat evenly.

SUBSTITUTION: *Although Italian sausage goes quite nicely in this salad, you could use another kind of cooked ground meat: Try pork, beef, or turkey. Just be sure to drain the meat before adding it to the salad.*

Sicilian Salad

SERVES 6

¼ CUP BALSAMIC VINEGAR

2 TEASPOONS DIJON MUSTARD

½ CUP OLIVE OIL

¾ POUND HARD SALAMI, CUT INTO
½-INCH CUBES

¾ POUND HARD CHEESE, SUCH AS MILD
PROVOLONE, GRUYÈRE, OR
CHEDDAR, CUT INTO ½-INCH CUBES

3 JARRED ROASTED RED PEPPERS, DICED

4 SCALLIONS, THINLY SLICED

2 TABLESPOONS CHOPPED FRESH BASIL,
OR 2 TEASPOONS DRIED

⅛ TEASPOON SALT

⅛ TEASPOON BLACK PEPPER

1 SMALL HEAD OF LETTUCE, LEAVES
SEPARATED, WASHED AND SPUN DRY

1. In a large bowl, whisk together the vinegar, mustard, and oil until well blended.

2. Add the salami, cheese, roasted peppers, scallions, basil, salt, and pepper. Toss well to combine and coat evenly with the dressing.

3. Line individual serving plates with the lettuce leaves. Toss the salad again and spoon it onto the lined plates, forming a slight mound.

Chinese Chicken Slaw

SERVES 4

♡ LOW-FAT

¾ CUP RICE WINE VINEGAR OR RED WINE VINEGAR

2 TABLESPOONS REDUCED-SODIUM SOY SAUCE

1 TABLESPOON ORIENTAL (DARK) SESAME OIL

1 TABLESPOON SUGAR

1 GARLIC CLOVE, MINCED

1 TEASPOON MINCED FRESH GINGER

1½ CUPS CHOPPED COOKED CHICKEN

2 CUPS PACKAGED COLESLAW MIX (CABBAGE AND CARROTS)

½ CUP DICED YELLOW OR RED BELL PEPPER

ONE 8-OUNCE CAN SLICED WATER CHESTNUTS, DRAINED

1. In a large serving bowl, whisk together the vinegar, soy sauce, sesame oil, sugar, garlic, and ginger until blended.

2. Add the chicken, coleslaw mix, bell pepper, and water chestnuts and toss well to combine and coat evenly with the dressing.

KITCHEN NOTE: *Chicken salad is a perfect way to use leftover roast chicken, or you can purchase whole roasted chickens from most large supermarkets, either from the deli or the packaged meat section.*

COBB SALAD

SERVES 4

1 POUND SKINLESS, BONELESS CHICKEN
    BREAST HALVES
½ POUND BACON, CUT INTO 2-INCH
    PIECES
1 RIPE AVOCADO, PEELED, PITTED, AND
    SLICED
1 LARGE TOMATO, SEEDED AND DICED
3 OUNCES BLUE CHEESE, CRUMBLED

⅛ TEASPOON SALT
¼ TEASPOON BLACK PEPPER
½ CUP BOTTLED RED WINE
    VINAIGRETTE
1 SMALL HEAD OF LEAFY RED OR GREEN
    LETTUCE, LEAVES SEPARATED,
    WASHED AND SPUN DRY

1. Bring a large skillet of water to a boil. Add the chicken breasts and simmer until no longer pink, about 10 minutes.

2. Meanwhile, cook the bacon in a medium skillet over medium heat until crisp, about 7 minutes. Drain the bacon on paper towels.

3. Drain the chicken, cool slightly, and shred.

4. In a large bowl, combine the chicken, bacon, avocado, tomato, blue cheese, salt, and pepper. Pour the dressing over the salad and toss well to combine and coat evenly.

5. Line individual serving plates with the lettuce leaves. Toss the salad again and spoon it onto the lined plates, forming a slight mound.

KITCHEN NOTE: *The Cobb salad was invented in 1926 at the Brown Derby Restaurant in Los Angeles by the owner, Bob Cobb, who was searching for a way to use up leftovers. The original salad included chopped avocado, lettuce, celery, tomato, bacon, chicken, hard-boiled egg, watercress, and blue cheese.*

Herbed Chicken Salad

SERVES 4

1 TABLESPOON OLIVE OIL

1¼ POUNDS SKINLESS, BONELESS
CHICKEN BREAST HALVES

¼ CUP DRY WHITE WINE OR CHICKEN
BROTH

½ CUP MAYONNAISE

2 TABLESPOONS FRESH LEMON JUICE

2 GARLIC CLOVES, MINCED

1½ TEASPOONS CHOPPED FRESH
ROSEMARY, OR ½ TEASPOON DRIED

½ TEASPOON HOT PEPPER SAUCE, OR
TO TASTE

4 MEDIUM SCALLIONS, THINLY SLICED

1 CELERY RIB, FINELY CHOPPED

½ CUP STRIPS OF OIL-PACKED SUN-
DRIED TOMATOES, DRAINED

¼ TEASPOON SALT

1. In a large skillet, warm the oil over medium-high heat. Add the chicken to the skillet and cook until browned, about 2 minutes per side. Add the wine. Reduce the heat to medium, cover, and cook until chicken is no longer pink, about 4 minutes. Drain the chicken and cool slightly.

2. Meanwhile, in a large bowl, mix the mayonnaise, lemon juice, garlic, rosemary, and hot pepper sauce. Add the scallions, celery, sun-dried tomatoes, and salt to the bowl and toss well to combine and coat evenly with the dressing.

3. Transfer the chicken to a cutting board and thinly slice it across the grain. Add the chicken to the salad and toss to combine.

Warm Pecan Chicken Salad

SERVES 4

⅔ CUP CHICKEN BROTH, PREFERABLY
    REDUCED-SODIUM
1 POUND SKINLESS, BONELESS CHICKEN
    BREAST HALVES
1 FIRM RIPE PEAR, CUT INTO 1-INCH
    CHUNKS
¼ CUP CHOPPED RED ONION
½ CUP RAISINS

½ CUP CHOPPED TOASTED PECANS
2 TABLESPOONS OLIVE OIL
2 TABLESPOONS BALSAMIC VINEGAR
2 TEASPOONS HONEY MUSTARD
½ TEASPOON SALT
¼ TEASPOON BLACK PEPPER

1. In a large skillet, bring the broth to a simmer over medium-high heat. Add the chicken, cover, and cook over medium heat until no longer pink, about 4 minutes per side.

2. Meanwhile, in a large bowl, combine the pear, onion, raisins, pecans, oil, vinegar, mustard, salt, and pepper.

3. Drain the chicken, cool slightly, and shred. Add the chicken to the salad and toss well to combine. Serve warm.

KITCHEN NOTE: *To toast pecans, preheat the oven to 350°. Spread pecan halves in a single layer on a baking sheet and toast in the oven for 7 to 10 minutes. Remove from the oven, cool slightly, and chop.*

Smoked Turkey and Potato Salad

SERVES 4

LOW-FAT

1 POUND SMALL UNPEELED RED
POTATOES, SCRUBBED AND CUT INTO
½-INCH CHUNKS

ONE 1-POUND PIECE OF SMOKED
TURKEY BREAST

½ CUP LOOSELY PACKED FRESH
CILANTRO

2 SCALLIONS

2 CUPS FRESH OR FROZEN CORN
KERNELS, THAWED

½ CUP REDUCED-FAT BOTTLED WHITE
OR RED WINE VINAIGRETTE

1 SMALL HEAD OF RED LEAFY LETTUCE,
LEAVES SEPARATED, WASHED AND
SPUN DRY

I. Steam the potatoes in a steamer set over 1 inch of boiling water, covered, until just tender, about 12 minutes.

2. Meanwhile, cut the turkey into bite-size pieces. Chop the cilantro. Thinly slice the scallions.

3. Transfer the potatoes to a large serving bowl. Add the turkey, cilantro, scallions, and corn. Pour the dressing over the salad and toss well to combine and coat evenly.

4. Line individual serving plates with the lettuce leaves. Toss the salad again and spoon it onto the lined plates, forming a slight mound.

Turkey Waldorf Salad

SERVES 6

♡ LOW-FAT

½ CUP REDUCED-FAT MAYONNAISE

¼ CUP PLAIN LOW-FAT YOGURT

1 TABLESPOON FRESH LEMON JUICE

1 TEASPOON DIJON MUSTARD

½ TEASPOON SALT

½ TEASPOON BLACK PEPPER

4 CUPS CUBED COOKED TURKEY
(ABOUT 1¾ POUNDS)

2 MEDIUM UNPEELED GRANNY SMITH
APPLES, DICED

2 CELERY RIBS, CHOPPED

⅓ CUP CHOPPED WALNUTS

3 TABLESPOONS MINCED FRESH PARSLEY

1. In a medium bowl, whisk together the mayonnaise, yogurt, lemon juice, mustard, salt, and pepper.

2. Add the turkey, apples, celery, walnuts, and parsley to the bowl and toss well to combine and coat evenly with the dressing.

Variation: *The flavor of this salad is easily altered by changing the combination of fruit and nuts. For instance, omit the apples and walnuts and add 1 cup halved seedless grapes and ½ cup toasted sliced almonds, or one 11-ounce can drained mandarin oranges and ½ cup chopped dry-roasted cashews.*

SHRiMP CAESAR SALAD

SERVES 4

1 POUND LARGE UNPEELED SHRIMP

1 LARGE HEAD OF ROMAINE LETTUCE, WASHED AND SPUN DRY

3 TABLESPOONS FRESH LEMON JUICE

1 TEASPOON DIJON MUSTARD

1 TEASPOON WORCESTERSHIRE SAUCE

3 CANNED ANCHOVY FILLETS, DRAINED AND MINCED, OR 1 TEASPOON ANCHOVY PASTE

2 GARLIC CLOVES, MINCED

¼ TEASPOON BLACK PEPPER

6 TABLESPOONS OLIVE OIL

⅓ CUP GRATED PARMESAN CHEESE

1 CUP CROUTONS

1. In a large saucepan of boiling water, cook the shrimp until pink, 1 to 2 minutes. Drain the shrimp, rinse under cold running water, and drain well. Peel the shrimp and put into a bowl of ice water.

2. Slice the lettuce leaves crosswise into ½-inch-wide strips or tear into bite-size pieces. Put the lettuce in a large serving bowl.

3. In a small bowl, mix the lemon juice, mustard, Worcestershire sauce, anchovies, garlic, and pepper until well blended. Slowly whisk in the oil until well blended and thickened. Pour the dressing over the lettuce and toss well to coat evenly.

4. Drain the shrimp and pat dry. Add the shrimp, grated cheese, and croutons to the salad and toss well to combine.

VARIATION: *Caesar salad is a natural for all sorts of toppings. Try adding sliced grilled chicken breasts, swordfish or tuna steaks, or cooked cubed potatoes or pasta.*

Mediterranean Tuna Salad

SERVES 6

¼ CUP RED WINE VINEGAR

2 TEASPOONS DIJON MUSTARD

2 GARLIC CLOVES, MINCED

⅓ CUP OLIVE OIL

ONE 15-OUNCE CAN SMALL WHITE
  BEANS, RINSED AND DRAINED

ONE 12-OUNCE CAN WATER-PACKED
  WHITE TUNA, DRAINED AND FLAKED

6 SCALLIONS, CHOPPED

3 CELERY RIBS, CHOPPED

2 TABLESPOONS CHOPPED FRESH DILL,
  OR 2 TEASPOONS DRIED

¼ TEASPOON SALT

¼ TEASPOON BLACK PEPPER

1 SMALL HEAD OF BOSTON LETTUCE,
  LEAVES SEPARATED, WASHED AND
  SPUN DRY

1. In a large serving bowl, whisk together the vinegar, mustard, and garlic. Slowly whisk in the oil until blended.

2. Add the beans, tuna, scallions, celery, dill, salt, and pepper to the bowl. Toss well to combine and coat evenly with the dressing.

3. Line individual serving plates with the lettuce leaves. Toss the salad again and spoon it onto the lined plates, forming a slight mound.

VARIATION: *This tuna salad mixture is also good stuffed into pita pockets with shredded lettuce and tomato slices, or spooned into hollow tomato halves.*

Ziti, Salmon, and Green Bean Salad

SERVES 4

½ POUND ZITI OR OTHER MEDIUM
    TUBULAR PASTA
2 CUPS FRESH GREEN BEANS, CUT
    DIAGONALLY INTO 1½-INCH
    LENGTHS
¼ CUP FRESH LEMON JUICE
2 TEASPOONS DIJON MUSTARD

2 TABLESPOONS CHOPPED FRESH DILL,
    OR 2 TEASPOONS DRIED
⅓ CUP OLIVE OIL
ONE 7½-OUNCE CAN SALMON,
    DRAINED AND FLAKED
¼ TEASPOON SALT
¼ TEASPOON BLACK PEPPER

1. In a large pot of boiling water, cook the pasta until al dente according to the package directions. Add the beans to the boiling water for the last 5 minutes of cooking.

2. Meanwhile, in a large serving bowl, whisk together the lemon juice, mustard, and dill. Slowly whisk in the oil until well blended.

3. Drain the pasta and beans, rinse under cold running water, and drain well.

4. Transfer the pasta and beans to the bowl and add the salmon. Season with the salt and pepper and toss well to combine and coat evenly with the dressing.

SWEET AFTERTHOUGHT: *For an easy dessert that is refreshing and pretty, try this: Fill canned peach halves with mashed fresh raspberries mixed with a little sugar. Top with whipped cream.*

Thai Noodle and Vegetable Salad

SERVES 4

½ POUND VERMICELLI

⅓ CUP PEANUT OIL

3 TABLESPOONS FRESH LEMON JUICE

2 TABLESPOONS BOTTLED TERIYAKI
SAUCE

1 TABLESPOON CREAMY PEANUT BUTTER

1 TEASPOON RICE WINE VINEGAR

1 CUP SHREDDED CARROTS

½ CUP CHOPPED CUCUMBER

⅓ CUP SLICED SCALLIONS

⅓ CUP LOOSELY PACKED FRESH
CILANTRO, COARSELY CHOPPED

1. In a large pot of boiling water, cook the pasta until al dente according to the package directions.

2. Meanwhile, in a large serving bowl, mix the oil, lemon juice, teriyaki sauce, peanut butter, and vinegar until well blended.

3. Drain the pasta, rinse under cold running water, and drain well. Transfer the pasta to the serving bowl. Add the carrots, cucumber, scallions, and cilantro to the pasta. Toss well to combine and coat evenly with the dressing.

SWEET AFTERTHOUGHT: *For a refreshing finish to this main dish salad, serve gingered pear sorbet. In a blender, purée one 29-ounce can of Bartlett pears with light syrup and 1 tablespoon chopped candied ginger. Pour the mixture into an 8-inch square pan and freeze until set. Scrape the mixture into stemmed glasses and serve.*

California Pasta Salad

SERVES 4

♡ LOW-FAT

½ POUND TRICOLOR PASTA TWISTS
¼ POUND SNOW PEAS, STRINGS
    REMOVED AND CUT DIAGONALLY
    INTO THIRDS
1 MEDIUM CUCUMBER

1 RIPE KIWI
1 CUP SEEDLESS RED GRAPES
1 CUP CHOPPED FRESH SPINACH LEAVES
½ CUP REDUCED-FAT BOTTLED POPPY
    SEED DRESSING

1. In a large pot of boiling water, cook the pasta until al dente according to the package directions. Add the snow peas for the last minute of cooking.

2. Meanwhile, peel, seed, and chop the cucumber. Peel and chop the kiwi. Cut the grapes in half. Set aside.

3. Drain the pasta and snow peas, rinse under cold running water, and drain well.

4. Transfer the pasta and snow peas to a large serving bowl. Add the spinach, cucumber, kiwi, and grapes.

5. Pour the dressing over the salad and toss well to combine and coat evenly.

KITCHEN NOTE: *To remove the strings from the pea pods: Break off the stem end and pull the string down the pod. Turn the pod and break off the tail, pulling the string down the other side.*

PASTA, PIZZA — PRONTO

Pasta with Fresh Tomato-Garlic Sauce

SERVES 4

¾ POUND LINGUINE
4 LARGE TOMATOES, CHOPPED
3 TABLESPOONS OLIVE OIL
2 GARLIC CLOVES, MINCED
¼ CUP CHOPPED FRESH BASIL, OR
   1 TABLESPOON DRIED

½ TEASPOON DRIED OREGANO
1 TEASPOON SALT
⅓ CUP GRATED PARMESAN CHEESE
CROUTONS, FOR GARNISH (OPTIONAL)

1. In a large pot of boiling water, cook the pasta until al dente according to the package directions.

2. Meanwhile, in a large serving bowl, combine the tomatoes, oil, garlic, basil, oregano, and salt.

3. Drain the pasta and add it to the bowl with the tomato mixture. Sprinkle with the Parmesan cheese and croutons, if desired, and serve.

KITCHEN NOTE: *To cook pasta properly, use about 4 quarts of water per pound. Be sure the water comes to a rapid boil before adding the pasta, and once added, stir occasionally to prevent the noodles from sticking together and to ensure even cooking.*

FETTUCCINE CARBONARA

SERVES 4

¾ POUND FETTUCCINE OR OTHER
    BROAD NOODLES
1½ CUPS FROZEN PEAS
4 SLICES BACON, CUT INTO 1-INCH
    PIECES
¾ CUP CHICKEN BROTH, PREFERABLY
    REDUCED-SODIUM

1 GARLIC CLOVE, MINCED
¾ CUP MILK OR HALF-AND-HALF
1 TABLESPOON FLOUR
½ CUP GRATED PARMESAN CHEESE
1 TABLESPOON UNSALTED BUTTER
½ TEASPOON BLACK PEPPER

1. In a large pot of boiling water, cook the fettuccine until al dente according to the package directions. Add the peas to the pot for the last 5 minutes of cooking.

2. Meanwhile, cook the bacon in a medium skillet over medium heat until crisp, about 7 minutes. Transfer the bacon to paper towels. Pour off the drippings from the skillet.

3. Drain the pasta and peas and return them to the pot.

4. Return the bacon to the skillet and add the broth and garlic. Cover and cook over medium heat for 2 minutes.

5. In a small cup, blend the milk and flour. Stir into the simmering broth mixture and simmer, stirring constantly, until slightly thickened, 1 to 2 minutes. Pour the mixture over the pasta and peas in the pot. Add the cheese, butter, and pepper, and toss well to coat evenly.

Penne with Sun-Dried Tomatoes and Artichokes

SERVES 4

1 TABLESPOON OLIVE OIL

1 MEDIUM ONION, CHOPPED

2 GARLIC CLOVES, MINCED

ONE 16-OUNCE CAN ITALIAN PLUM
   TOMATOES, CHOPPED, JUICE
   RESERVED

⅓ CUP STRIPS OF OIL-PACKED SUN-
   DRIED TOMATOES, DRAINED

2 TEASPOONS DRIED BASIL

1 TEASPOON DRIED OREGANO

¾ POUND PENNE OR OTHER MEDIUM
   TUBULAR PASTA

ONE 14½-OUNCE JAR MARINATED
   ARTICHOKE HEARTS

¼ CUP GRATED PARMESAN CHEESE

1. Bring a large pot of water to a boil over high heat.

2. Meanwhile, in a large deep skillet, warm the oil over medium heat. Add the onion and garlic and sauté until the onion is softened, about 3 minutes. Add the canned tomatoes with the juice, the sun-dried tomatoes, basil, and oregano. Simmer the sauce, stirring occasionally, until slightly thickened, about 6 minutes.

3. While the sauce simmers, cook the pasta in the boiling water until al dente according to the package directions.

4. Add the artichoke hearts with their marinade to the skillet and simmer until heated through, 3 to 4 minutes.

5. Drain the pasta, add it to the skillet, and toss well to combine and coat. Transfer the pasta mixture to a large shallow serving bowl, sprinkle with the Parmesan cheese, and serve.

GREEK-STYLE PASTA

SERVES 6

⅓ CUP OLIVE OIL

3 GARLIC CLOVES, CRUSHED

1 POUND FETTUCCINE OR OTHER
BROAD NOODLES

¼ CUP FRESH LEMON JUICE

¼ POUND FETA CHEESE, CRUMBLED
(1 CUP)

½ CUP PITTED BLACK OLIVES

1 TEASPOON DRIED OREGANO

1. Bring a large pot of water to a boil over high heat.

2. Meanwhile, in a medium skillet, warm the oil over medium heat. Add the garlic and sauté until golden, about 5 minutes. Discard the garlic. Keep the oil warm over low heat.

3. Cook the pasta in the boiling water until al dente according to the package directions.

4. Drain the pasta and transfer it to a large serving bowl.

5. Pour the warm olive oil over the pasta and add the lemon juice, feta cheese, olives, and oregano. Toss well to combine and coat evenly. Serve hot, or at room temperature.

KITCHEN NOTE: *Adding salt to the pasta cooking water will add flavor to the pasta, but unsalted water will reach a boil faster. So if desired, add salt to the water after it reaches a boil and before you add the pasta.*

Rigatoni with Eggplant Sauce

SERVES 4

♡ LOW-FAT

1 TABLESPOON OLIVE OIL
1 SMALL EGGPLANT, CUT INTO ½-INCH
    CUBES
2 GARLIC CLOVES, MINCED
1 TEASPOON DRIED ROSEMARY
ONE 16-OUNCE CAN ITALIAN PLUM
    TOMATOES, CHOPPED, JUICE
    RESERVED

½ TEASPOON SALT
¼ TEASPOON BLACK PEPPER
12 OUNCES RIGATONI OR OTHER
    MEDIUM TUBULAR PASTA

1. Bring a large pot of water to a boil over high heat.

2. Meanwhile, in a large nonstick skillet, warm the oil over medium-high heat. Add the eggplant and cook, stirring frequently, until softened and beginning to brown, about 6 minutes.

3. Add the garlic and rosemary to the skillet and sauté for 1 minute. Stir in the tomatoes with the reserved juice, salt, and pepper, and simmer, uncovered, until slightly thickened, about 8 minutes.

4. While the sauce simmers, cook the pasta in the boiling water until al dente according to the package directions.

5. Drain the pasta and return it to the pot. Add the eggplant mixture and toss well to combine and coat. Transfer the pasta to a large shallow bowl to serve.

PASTA PUTTANESCA

SERVES 6

½ CUP OLIVE OIL

6 OIL-PACKED ANCHOVY FILLETS, DRAINED, OR 2 TEASPOONS ANCHOVY PASTE

3 GARLIC CLOVES, MINCED

½ TEASPOON CRUSHED RED PEPPER FLAKES

ONE 28-OUNCE CAN PEELED PLUM TOMATOES, DRAINED AND CHOPPED

¾ CUP PITTED BLACK OLIVES

3 TABLESPOONS DRAINED CAPERS

1 TEASPOON DRIED OREGANO

¼ CUP CHOPPED FRESH PARSLEY

¼ TEASPOON BLACK PEPPER

1 POUND VERMICELLI OR SPAGHETTI

1. Bring a large pot of water to a boil over high heat.

2. Meanwhile, in a large skillet, warm the oil over medium heat. Add the anchovies, garlic, and red pepper flakes and cook, stirring often, for 1 minute. Stir in the tomatoes, olives, capers, oregano, parsley, and pepper, and cook over medium heat, stirring occasionally, for 10 minutes.

3. While the sauce simmers, cook the pasta in the boiling water until al dente according to the package directions.

4. Drain the pasta and transfer it to a large serving bowl. Add the sauce and toss well to combine and coat evenly.

KITCHEN NOTE: *The popularity of the spicy pasta puttanesca is widespread. Legend has it that the dish was a favorite of the Roman "ladies of the evening," for whom it is named, because it was so quickly made.*

Penne with Summer Vegetables

SERVES 6

½ cup olive oil

1 medium eggplant, cut into 1½-inch cubes

1 medium yellow summer squash, cut in half lengthwise, then sliced crosswise ¼ inch thick

1 medium zucchini, cut in half lengthwise, then sliced crosswise ¼ inch thick

4 plum tomatoes, coarsely chopped

1 teaspoon dried basil

1 teaspoon dried oregano

1 teaspoon salt

1 pound penne or other medium tubular pasta

¼ cup grated Parmesan cheese

1. Bring a large pot of water to a boil over high heat.

2. Meanwhile, in a large deep skillet, warm ¼ cup of the oil over medium-high heat. Add the eggplant, yellow squash, zucchini, tomatoes, basil, oregano, and salt and cook, stirring frequently, until the vegetables are softened, about 10 minutes.

3. Cook the pasta in the boiling water until al dente according to the package directions.

4. Add the remaining ¼ cup of oil to the skillet and stir well to combine.

5. Drain the pasta and transfer it to a large serving bowl. Add the vegetable mixture and toss to mix and coat. Add the cheese and toss again.

Chicken Tortellini with Tomato-Cheese Sauce

SERVES 4

3 TABLESPOONS UNSALTED BUTTER

½ CUP FINELY CHOPPED ONION

3 TABLESPOONS FLOUR

2 TEASPOONS DRY MUSTARD

1¼ CUPS MILK

1¼ CUPS SHREDDED SHARP CHEDDAR CHEESE

¾ POUND CHICKEN-FILLED TORTELLINI

6 PLUM TOMATOES, CHOPPED

¼ CUP GRATED PARMESAN CHEESE

1. Bring a large pot of water to a boil over high heat.

2. Meanwhile, in a medium saucepan, melt the butter over medium heat. Add the onion and sauté until softened, about 3 minutes. Stir in the flour and mustard until blended and cook, stirring often, until no longer visible. Whisk in the milk until blended. Cook, whisking constantly, until it just begins to boil. Reduce the heat to medium-low and cook, whisking frequently, until thickened, 5

to 7 minutes. Add the Cheddar and stir until melted and the sauce is smooth. Remove the pan from the heat.

3. Add the tortellini to the boiling water and cook until al dente according to the package directions.

4. Drain the tortellini and transfer it to a large serving bowl. Add the cheese sauce, tomatoes, and grated Parmesan and toss well to coat evenly.

Bow Ties with Sausage and Smoked Mozzarella

SERVES 6

½ POUND HOT OR SWEET ITALIAN
    SAUSAGE, CASINGS REMOVED
1 TABLESPOON OLIVE OIL
2 GARLIC CLOVES, MINCED
1 TABLESPOON TOMATO PASTE
ONE 16-OUNCE CAN WHOLE
    TOMATOES, CHOPPED, JUICE
    RESERVED

¾ POUND BOW TIE PASTA OR OTHER
    FANCY PASTA SHAPE
½ POUND SMOKED MOZZARELLA, CUT
    INTO ½-INCH CUBES
¼ TEASPOON SALT
¼ TEASPOON BLACK PEPPER

1. Bring a large pot of water to a boil over high heat.

2. Meanwhile, in a large nonstick skillet, brown the sausage over medium-high heat, stirring to break up with a large spoon, about 7 minutes. Transfer the sausage to paper towels to drain. Pour off the drippings from the skillet.

3. Warm the oil in the skillet over medium heat. Return the sausage to the skillet and add the garlic. Cook, stirring frequently, for 30 seconds. Stir in the tomato paste, then add the tomatoes with the reserved juice. Bring to

a simmer over medium heat and simmer until thickened, about 5 minutes. Keep warm over low heat.

4. While the sauce simmers, cook the pasta in the boiling water until al dente according to the package directions.

5. Drain the pasta and return it to the pot. Add the sausage mixture and toss well to combine and coat evenly. Add the smoked mozzarella and toss gently to combine. Season with salt and pepper. Transfer to a large serving bowl.

Egg Noodles with Pork and Mushroom Cream Sauce

SERVES 4

½ OUNCE DRIED PORCINI MUSHROOMS

1 CUP HOT CHICKEN BROTH,
PREFERABLY REDUCED-SODIUM

½ POUND MEDIUM-WIDTH EGG
NOODLES

1 TABLESPOON VEGETABLE OIL

¾ POUND PORK TENDERLOIN, HALVED
LENGTHWISE, THEN CUT CROSSWISE
INTO ¼-INCH-WIDE SLICES

1 TABLESPOON UNSALTED BUTTER

⅓ CUP MINCED SHALLOTS

2 CUPS HALF-AND-HALF

¼ TEASPOON SALT

¼ TEASPOON BLACK PEPPER

1. In a small bowl, combine the mushrooms and chicken broth. Let stand until the mushrooms are softened, about 10 minutes.

2. In a large pot of boiling water, cook the egg noodles until al dente according to the package directions.

3. Meanwhile, in large deep skillet, warm the oil over medium-high heat. Add the pork and sauté just until cooked through, about 5 minutes. Transfer the pork to a plate. Warm the butter in the skillet over medium-high heat until melted. Add the shallots and sauté until softened, about 3 minutes.

4. Drain the egg noodles and return them to the pot.

5. Drain the mushrooms, reserving the liquid, and coarsely chop. Add to the skillet and sauté for 1 minute. Strain the broth through a fine sieve into the skillet, increase the heat to medium-high, and simmer for 1 minute. Add the half-and-half and simmer until the sauce has thickened and is reduced by half, about 8 minutes. Season with the salt and pepper.

6. Add the pork and noodles to the skillet, toss well to combine, and heat through.

Spaghetti with Ground Meat Sauce

SERVES 6

½ POUND LEAN GROUND BEEF
½ POUND GROUND PORK
1 TEASPOON OLIVE OIL
2 MEDIUM ONIONS, THINLY SLICED
2 GARLIC CLOVES, MINCED
1 TABLESPOON TOMATO PASTE
ONE 28-OUNCE CAN WHOLE
   TOMATOES, DRAINED AND CHOPPED

⅔ CUP CHICKEN BROTH, PREFERABLY
   REDUCED-SODIUM
2 TEASPOONS DRIED OREGANO
½ TEASPOON CRUSHED RED PEPPER
   FLAKES
¼ TEASPOON SALT
¾ POUND SPAGHETTI

1. Bring a large pot of water to a boil over high heat.

2. Meanwhile, in a large nonstick skillet, brown the beef and pork over medium-high heat, breaking up the meat with a spoon, about 5 minutes. Transfer the meat to a plate. Pour off the drippings from the skillet.

3. Warm the oil in the skillet over medium-high heat. Add the onions and garlic and cook, stirring occasionally, until softened, about 5 minutes. Stir in the tomato paste, then the tomatoes, chicken broth, oregano,

red pepper flakes, and salt. Return the browned meat to the skillet. Simmer the mixture over medium-low heat, stirring occasionally, until the sauce has thickened slightly, about 8 minutes.

4. While the sauce simmers, cook the pasta in the boiling water until al dente according to the package directions.

5. Drain the pasta and return it to the pot. Add the meat sauce and toss well to combine. Transfer the pasta to a large serving bowl.

KOREAN BEEF AND NOODLE
STIR-FRY

SERVES 4

¼ CUP SOY SAUCE

2 GARLIC CLOVES, MINCED

1 TABLESPOON ORIENTAL (DARK)
   SESAME OIL

1 TEASPOON SUGAR

½ POUND BEEF ROUND STIR-FRY
   STRIPS, CUT IN HALF CROSSWISE

1 LARGE CARROT

1 MEDIUM ONION

½ POUND NAPA CABBAGE

¼ POUND FRESH SHIITAKE
   MUSHROOMS, STEMMED

¼ CUP VEGETABLE OIL, PREFERABLY
   PEANUT OIL

½ POUND VERMICELLI, BROKEN INTO
   THIRDS

1 TABLESPOON TOASTED SESAME SEEDS
   (OPTIONAL)

1. In a small bowl, blend the soy sauce, garlic, sesame oil, and sugar. Add the meat and set aside.

2. Bring a large pot of water to a boil over high heat.

3. Meanwhile, peel and thinly slice the carrot. Keeping vegetables separate, thinly slice the onion, cabbage, and mushroom caps. Set aside.

4. In a large heavy skillet or wok, warm 2 tablespoons of the oil over high heat. Add the carrot and stir-fry until beginning to soften, about 30 seconds. Add the onion and stir-fry until beginning to soften, about 30 seconds.

Add cabbage and stir-fry until wilted, about 1 minute. Transfer the vegetables to a plate.

5. Cook the pasta in the boiling water until al dente according to the package directions.

6. While the pasta cooks, warm the remaining 2 tablespoons of oil in the skillet over medium-high heat. Add the beef with the liquid and the mushrooms and cook, stirring frequently, until the meat is browned and the mushrooms are tender, 3 to 4 minutes.

7. Drain the pasta and add it to the skillet along with the reserved vegetables. Toss well to combine, then heat through. Sprinkle with sesame seeds, if desired.

Pasta with Turkey Bolognese

SERVES 4

12 OUNCES GROUND TURKEY
ONE 26-OUNCE JAR SPAGHETTI SAUCE
1 TEASPOON DRIED BASIL
½ TEASPOON DRIED ROSEMARY

2 MEDIUM ZUCCHINI, CUT IN HALF
LENGTHWISE, THEN SLICED
CROSSWISE
¾ POUND MEDIUM PASTA SHELLS
¼ CUP GRATED PARMESAN CHEESE

1. Bring a large pot of water to a boil over high heat.

2. Meanwhile, in a large nonstick skillet, brown the turkey over medium heat, breaking up the meat with a spoon, about 5 minutes.

3. Stir in the spaghetti sauce, basil, and rosemary. Bring the mixture to a boil over medium-high heat and add the zucchini. Reduce the heat to medium-low, cover, and simmer until the zucchini is tender, about 5 minutes.

4. While the sauce simmers, cook the pasta in the boiling water until al dente according to the package directions.

5. Drain the pasta and transfer it to a large serving bowl. Add the sauce and toss well to coat. Add the Parmesan cheese and toss again.

KITCHEN NOTE: *Get a head start on another meal by cooking twice as much pasta as you need. Rinse the pasta you won't be using right away under cold running water and drain well. Toss with a little olive oil and store airtight in the refrigerator for up to three days. Steam over boiling water to reheat.*

Spinach Pasta with Pesto and Ham

SERVES 4

¾ POUND SPINACH LINGUINE

½ CUP READY-MADE PESTO

¼ CUP HALF-AND-HALF

½ POUND SLICED BOILED HAM,
STACKED AND CUT CROSSWISE INTO
THIN STRIPS

1 PINT CHERRY TOMATOES, QUARTERED

¼ CUP GRATED ROMANO OR PARMESAN
CHEESE

1. In a large pot of boiling water, cook the pasta until al dente according to the package directions.

2. Drain the pasta and return it to the pot. Add the pesto and half-and-half and toss well to coat evenly. Add the ham and tomatoes and gently toss again to mix.

3. Transfer to a large serving bowl and sprinkle with the grated cheese.

Kitchen Note: *The best way to test pasta for doneness is to bite into a small piece. Cooking pasta until al dente means cooking it until tender but still firm to the bite. Also, remember that pasta will continue to cook from residual heat for a few seconds after it is drained, so be careful not to boil it too long.*

Fettuccine with Curried Chicken

SERVES 4

1 TABLESPOON UNSALTED BUTTER

1 TABLESPOON OLIVE OIL

¾ POUND SKINLESS, BONELESS
CHICKEN BREAST HALVES, CUT INTO
BITE-SIZE PIECES

¼ CUP CHICKEN BROTH, PREFERABLY
REDUCED-SODIUM

1 TEASPOON CURRY POWDER

½ CUP HALF-AND-HALF

¾ POUND FETTUCCINE OR OTHER
BROAD NOODLES

¼ TEASPOON SALT

¼ TEASPOON BLACK PEPPER

1. Bring a large pot of water to a boil over high heat.

2. Meanwhile, in a large skillet, warm the butter and the oil over medium-high heat. Add the chicken and sauté until opaque, about 5 minutes. Transfer the chicken to a plate.

3. Add the chicken broth to the skillet and bring to a boil over medium-high heat, stirring to scrape up any browned bits. Stir in the curry powder and half-and-half and simmer over medium heat until the sauce thickens, about 5 minutes.

4. While the sauce simmers, cook the pasta in the boiling water until al dente according to the package directions.

5. Return the chicken with any juices to the skillet and simmer, stirring occasionally, until heated through, about 2 minutes.

6. Drain the pasta and transfer it to a large shallow serving bowl. Pour the chicken mixture over the pasta and toss well to combine and coat evenly. Season with the salt and pepper.

Ziti with Tuna and Tomatoes

SERVES 4

3 TABLESPOONS OLIVE OIL

1 SMALL ONION, FINELY CHOPPED

2 MEDIUM GARLIC CLOVES, MINCED

ONE 28-OUNCE CAN PLUM TOMATOES, CHOPPED, JUICE RESERVED

¼ CUP DRY RED WINE (OPTIONAL)

ONE 6-OUNCE CAN WHITE TUNA, DRAINED AND FLAKED

⅓ CUP PITTED BLACK OLIVES

1 TABLESPOON BALSAMIC VINEGAR

2 TABLESPOONS CHOPPED FRESH PARSLEY

¼ TEASPOON BLACK PEPPER

¾ POUND ZITI OR OTHER MEDIUM TUBULAR PASTA

1. Bring a large pot of water to a boil over high heat.

2. Meanwhile, in a large skillet, warm the oil over medium heat. Add the onion and garlic and sauté until the onion is softened, about 3 minutes.

3. Add the tomatoes with the reserved juice and the wine, if desired, to the skillet. Bring to a boil over medium-high heat. Reduce the heat to medium and simmer, uncovered, until thickened slightly, about 5 minutes. Stir in the tuna, olives, vinegar, parsley, and pepper, and keep warm over low heat.

4. Cook the pasta in the boiling water until al dente according to the package directions.

5. Drain the pasta and transfer it to a large serving bowl. Add the tuna sauce and toss well to combine.

Linguine with Spicy Red Clam Sauce

SERVES 4

♡ LOW-FAT

2 TEASPOONS OLIVE OIL

2 GARLIC CLOVES, MINCED

2 TABLESPOONS TOMATO PASTE

ONE 8-OUNCE BOTTLE CLAM JUICE

TWO 6½-OUNCE CANS CHOPPED
   CLAMS, ½ CUP JUICE RESERVED

¾ POUND LINGUINE OR SPAGHETTI

2 TABLESPOONS CHOPPED FRESH
   PARSLEY

⅛ TEASPOON CRUSHED RED PEPPER
   FLAKES

¼ TEASPOON BLACK PEPPER

⅓ CUP GRATED PARMESAN CHEESE
   (OPTIONAL)

1. Bring a large pot of water to a boil over high heat.

2. Meanwhile, in a large nonstick skillet, warm the oil over medium heat. Add the garlic and sauté for 1 minute. Stir in the tomato paste and cook, stirring constantly, for 1 minute.

3. Add the clam juice and the ½ cup canned clam juice. Cook over medium heat, stirring occasionally, until slightly thickened, about 10 minutes.

4. While the sauce simmers, cook the pasta in the boiling water until al dente according to the package directions. Drain the pasta and return it to the pot.

5. Add the clams, parsley, red pepper flakes, and pepper to the skillet and heat through. Pour the mixture over the pasta and toss well to combine. Serve with the Parmesan cheese on the side, if desired.

Pasta Twists with Scallops and Leeks

SERVES 4

♡ LOW-FAT

¾ POUND ROTINI OR OTHER SHORT
    PASTA TWISTS

3 TABLESPOONS OLIVE OIL

1 GARLIC CLOVE, MINCED

2 MEDIUM LEEKS, TRIMMED, SPLIT
    LENGTHWISE, RINSED WELL, AND
    CHOPPED

1 POUND SEA SCALLOPS, HALVED OR
    QUARTERED DEPENDING ON SIZE

1 TABLESPOON ANISE-FLAVORED
    LIQUEUR (OPTIONAL)

1 TABLESPOON FRESH LEMON JUICE

2 TEASPOONS GRATED LEMON ZEST

¼ TEASPOON SALT

¼ TEASPOON BLACK PEPPER

1. In a large pot of boiling water, cook the pasta until al dente according to the package directions.

2. Meanwhile, in a large skillet, warm the oil over medium heat. Add the garlic and leeks and sauté until leeks are softened, about 5 minutes. Add the scallops and sauté until opaque in the center, 1 to 2 minutes. Add the liqueur, if desired, and cook for 30 seconds.

3. Drain the pasta and return it to the pot. Add the scallop mixture, lemon juice, and lemon zest and toss well to combine. Season with the salt and pepper and serve.

SWEET AFTERTHOUGHT: *Serve a light and refreshing dessert with this pasta dish. Purée frozen (unthawed) raspberries with a little sugar to taste. Combine with cut-up fresh ripe strawberries and spoon into serving glasses. Garnish with a sprig of fresh mint.*

SEAFOOD LO MEIN

SERVES 6

♡ LOW-FAT

¾ POUND FRESH THIN CHINESE
   NOODLES OR LINGUINE
⅓ CUP CHICKEN BROTH, PREFERABLY
   REDUCED-SODIUM
2 TABLESPOONS SOY SAUCE
1 TABLESPOON OYSTER SAUCE
1 TABLESPOON ORIENTAL (DARK)
   SESAME OIL
1 TEASPOON CORNSTARCH

1 TABLESPOON PLUS 2 TEASPOONS
   VEGETABLE OIL, PREFERABLY PEANUT
2 LARGE EGGS, BEATEN
½ POUND BAY SCALLOPS
1½ TABLESPOONS MINCED FRESH
   GINGER
1 SMALL RED ONION, HALVED
   CROSSWISE AND THINLY SLICED
½ POUND PEELED, COOKED SMALL
   SHRIMP

1. In a large pot of boiling water, cook the noodles until al dente according to the package directions.

2. Meanwhile, in a small bowl, blend the chicken broth, soy sauce, oyster sauce, 2 teaspoons of the sesame oil, and the cornstarch. Set aside.

3. Drain the noodles, rinse under cold running water, and drain well. Return the noodles to the pot and toss with the remaining teaspoon of sesame oil.

4. In a large skillet, warm 1 tablespoon of the vegetable oil over medium heat. Add the eggs and scramble until dry, about 1 minute. Transfer the eggs to a plate. Add the scallops and sauté until opaque, about 2 minutes. Transfer the scallops to the plate.

5. Warm the remaining 2 teaspoons of oil in the skillet over medium-high heat. Add the ginger and sauté for 30 seconds. Add the onion and sauté for about 3 minutes.

6. Stir the broth mixture and add to the skillet. Stir in the noodles and cook for 1 to 2 minutes, until the noodles are heated through and the sauce has thickened.

7. Return the eggs and scallops to the skillet and add the shrimp. Cook, stirring frequently, until heated through, about 1 minute. Serve hot.

Sausage and Spinach Pizza

SERVES 4

1 TEASPOON VEGETABLE OIL

¼ POUND SWEET OR HOT ITALIAN
TURKEY SAUSAGE, CASINGS
REMOVED

ONE 10-OUNCE TUBE REFRIGERATED
PIZZA CRUST

¾ CUP BOTTLED PIZZA SAUCE

ONE 10-OUNCE PACKAGE CHOPPED
SPINACH, THAWED AND DRAINED

1 CUP SHREDDED MOZZARELLA OR
PROVOLONE CHEESE

1. Preheat the oven to 425°. In a medium nonstick skillet, warm the oil over medium-high heat. Crumble the sausage into the skillet and brown, stirring frequently, for about 5 minutes. Transfer the sausage to paper towels to drain.

2. Lightly oil a 15½ x 10½-inch jelly-roll pan. Unroll the dough, transfer to the prepared pan, and press out to the edges. Pinch up the edges to make a rim.

3. Bake the crust until just beginning to brown, about 5 minutes.

4. Spread the pizza sauce over the partially baked crust. Sprinkle with the crumbled sausage and the spinach.

5. Bake for 10 minutes, until the crust is browned. Sprinkle with the cheese and bake for 2 minutes, until melted. Cut into squares and serve.

Mexican Pizza

SERVES 4

½ POUND LEAN GROUND BEEF
1 TABLESPOON PACKAGED TACO
    SEASONING
ONE 10-OUNCE TUBE REFRIGERATED
    PIZZA CRUST

1½ CUPS SHREDDED MONTEREY JACK
    CHEESE
1 MEDIUM TOMATO, DICED
½ CUP DICED PITTED BLACK OLIVES
⅓ CUP SLICED SCALLIONS

1. Preheat the oven to 450°. Crumble the beef into a large nonstick skillet and brown over medium-high heat, stirring frequently, about 5 minutes.

2. Drain off the drippings from the skillet, stir in the taco seasoning, and cook for 1 minute. Remove the skillet from the heat.

3. Lightly oil a 15½ x 10½-inch jelly-roll pan. Unroll the dough, transfer to the prepared pan, and press out to the edges. Pinch up the edges to make a rim.

4. Leaving a 1-inch border, spread the ground beef mixture over the crust. Sprinkle with the cheese, then the tomatoes and olives.

5. Bake for 10 minutes, or until the edge of the crust is browned and crisp and the cheese is melted.

6. Sprinkle the pizza with the scallions. Cut into squares and serve.

Broccoli and Ricotta Flatbread Pizza

SERVES 4

ONE 16-OUNCE FULLY BAKED ITALIAN
    FLATBREAD SHELL
ONE 10-OUNCE PACKAGE FROZEN
    CHOPPED BROCCOLI
ONE 8-OUNCE CONTAINER PART-SKIM
    RICOTTA CHEESE

¼ TEASPOON SALT
¼ TEASPOON BLACK PEPPER
1 CUP SHREDDED MOZZARELLA OR
    PROVOLONE CHEESE
1 TEASPOON CRUSHED RED PEPPER
    FLAKES (OPTIONAL)

1. Preheat the oven to 450°. Place the flatbread on a baking sheet.

2. Cook the broccoli according to the package directions. Drain well.

3. Leaving a 1-inch border, spread the ricotta cheese over the flatbread shell. Scatter the broccoli over the top. Sprinkle with the salt and pepper, then the mozzarella cheese.

4. Bake for 10 to 12 minutes, or until the edge of the crust is browned and crisp and the cheese is melted and bubbly.

5. Sprinkle the pizza with the red pepper flakes, if desired. Cut into wedges and serve.

Pesto, Potato, and Cheese Flatbread Pizza

SERVES 4

ONE 16-OUNCE FULLY BAKED ITALIAN
　FLATBREAD SHELL
3 TABLESPOONS READY-MADE PESTO
1½ CUPS SHREDDED MOZZARELLA
　CHEESE

1 MEDIUM UNPEELED RED POTATO,
　THINLY SLICED
¼ CUP JARRED ROASTED RED PEPPER
　STRIPS, DRAINED (OPTIONAL)
1 TABLESPOON OLIVE OIL

1. Preheat the oven to 450°. Place the flatbread shell on a baking sheet.

2. Leaving a 1-inch border, spread the pesto over the crust. Sprinkle with the cheese. Top with the potato slices and roasted red pepper strips, if desired. Drizzle with the oil.

3. Bake for 10 to 12 minutes, or until the edge of the crust is browned and crisp and the potatoes are tender.

4. Cut the pizza into wedges and serve.

English Muffin Mini-Pizzas

SERVES 4

4 ENGLISH MUFFINS, SPLIT
ONE 8-OUNCE CONTAINER PART-SKIM
   RICOTTA CHEESE
1 CUP BOTTLED SPAGHETTI SAUCE

½ CUP FINELY CHOPPED GREEN BELL
   PEPPER
1 CUP LOW-FAT SHREDDED SWISS
   CHEESE

1. Preheat the oven to 400°. Place the muffin halves on a baking sheet and toast in the oven for 5 minutes.

2. Spread 2 tablespoons of the ricotta cheese, then 2 tablespoons of the spaghetti sauce over each muffin half. Sprinkle with some of the peppers and the shredded cheese.

3. Bake the pizzas for 10 to 12 minutes, until heated through and the cheese is melted.

Variation: *The best part about these individual pizzas is that they can be made to order. For instance, instead of chopped green bell pepper you could use: chopped olives; drained, canned minced clams; thinly sliced zucchini or summer squash; or cooked ground turkey. Shredded Monterey Jack, Cheddar, or provolone cheese are also good substitutes.*

French Bread Pizzas

SERVES 4

½ POUND LEAN GROUND BEEF
ONE 1-POUND LOAF FRENCH BREAD
ONE 6-OUNCE CAN TOMATO PASTE
1 TEASPOON DRIED OREGANO

2 CUPS SLICED BUTTON MUSHROOMS
¼ CUP BOTTLED ITALIAN DRESSING
½ CUP SHREDDED MOZZARELLA CHEESE

1. Preheat the broiler. Line a broiler pan with foil.

2. In a large nonstick skillet, brown the beef over medium-high heat, breaking it up with a wooden spoon, about 5 minutes. Drain off all the fat.

3. Slice the bread in half lengthwise and place, cut sides up, on the broiler pan. Spread the tomato paste evenly over the tops and sprinkle with ½ teaspoon of the oregano. Top with the meat and mushrooms. Drizzle the salad dressing over the tops and sprinkle with the remaining oregano, then the cheese.

4. Broil 6 inches from the heat for 2 minutes, or until the cheese is melted. Cut into slices and serve.

Variations: *A number of different toppings can be used on this pizza. Try using thinly sliced onions, bell peppers, or pepperoni instead of the mushrooms, or crumbled cooked sausage in place of the ground beef.*

GRILLED AND BROILED

Spicy Cheddar Burgers

SERVES 4

1 TABLESPOON CHILI POWDER

1 TABLESPOON PAPRIKA

1 TEASPOON GARLIC POWDER

1 TEASPOON ONION POWDER

¾ TEASPOON SALT

½ TEASPOON GROUND CUMIN

½ TEASPOON BLACK PEPPER

1 POUND LEAN GROUND BEEF

4 SLICES SHARP CHEDDAR CHEESE

4 EGG-ENRICHED HAMBURGER BUNS,
   SPLIT

2 TABLESPOONS UNSALTED BUTTER, AT
   ROOM TEMPERATURE

1 SMALL RED ONION, THINLY SLICED

1. Preheat the broiler or prepare the grill. If broiling, line a broiler pan with foil.

2. In a small bowl, combine the chili powder, paprika, garlic powder, onion powder, salt, cumin, and pepper. Set aside.

3. Form the ground meat into four ¾-inch-thick patties. Sprinkle both sides of the patties with the spice mixture, coating evenly.

4. Arrange the burgers on the prepared broiler pan or grill. Broil or grill 4 inches from

the heat for 5 minutes. Turn the burgers over and cook for 1 minute, then top each with a slice of the cheese. Cook for 2 to 3 minutes for medium-rare meat, about 4 minutes for medium meat.

5. Meanwhile, grill or toast the hamburger buns. Brush the cut sides with the softened butter.

6. Set the burgers on the buns and top each one with slices of red onion.

KITCHEN NOTE: *When forming ground meat into patties (or meatballs), dampen your hands with a little water; this will prevent the meat from sticking to them.*

HORSERADISH BURGERS

SERVES 4

1 POUND LEAN GROUND BEEF
1 SMALL ONION, FINELY CHOPPED
1½ TABLESPOONS PREPARED
   HORSERADISH
1 TABLESPOON WORCESTERSHIRE
   SAUCE

1 TEASPOON SALT
1 TEASPOON BLACK PEPPER
4 KAISER ROLLS, SPLIT
¼ CUP KETCHUP
1 TABLESPOON PREPARED MUSTARD
1 TABLESPOON MAYONNAISE

1. Prepare the grill or preheat the broiler. If broiling, line a broiler pan with foil.

2. In a medium bowl, mix the ground beef with the onion, horseradish, Worcestershire sauce, salt, and pepper. Form the mixture into four ¾-inch-thick patties.

3. Arrange the burgers on the prepared broiler pan or the grill. Grill or broil 4 to 6 inches from the heat for about 5 minutes on each side for medium meat.

4. Meanwhile, grill or toast the rolls. In a small bowl, combine the ketchup, mustard, and mayonnaise.

5. Set the burgers on the rolls and top each one with some of the ketchup mixture.

GRILLED PEPPER STEAKS WITH SHIITAKE MUSHROOMS

SERVES 4

4 BEEF TENDERLOIN STEAKS (1 INCH
THICK, ABOUT 5 OUNCES EACH)
½ TEASPOON SALT
1 TABLESPOON COARSELY GROUND
BLACK PEPPERCORNS

¾ POUND FRESH SHIITAKE
MUSHROOMS, STEMMED
2 TEASPOONS OLIVE OIL

1. Preheat the broiler or prepare the grill. If broiling, line a broiler pan with foil and lightly oil the rack.

2. Season the meat lightly with the salt, then pat the pepper firmly onto both sides of the steaks. Set aside.

3. Thread the mushrooms onto 4 skewers by piercing through the center of each cap at an angle. Brush the mushrooms with the oil.

4. Arrange the steaks and mushroom skewers, cap side toward the heat, on the prepared broiler pan or the grill.

5. Broil or grill the steaks 4 inches from the heat 3 to 4 minutes per side for rare to medium-rare meat. Grill or broil the mushroom skewers until tender and lightly browned, about 3 minutes.

6. Serve each of the steaks with a skewer of mushrooms.

KITCHEN NOTE: *Fresh shiitake mushrooms have very large, meaty caps. The stems are too tough to eat, but you can use them to make stocks or sauces. Discard the stems after they have been used as a flavoring.*

BLACKENED FLANK STEAK

SERVES 4

1 TABLESPOON COARSELY GROUND
   BLACK PEPPER
2 TEASPOONS ONION POWDER
1½ TEASPOONS GARLIC POWDER
1 TEASPOON PAPRIKA
1 TEASPOON SALT

¾ TEASPOON WORCESTERSHIRE SAUCE
½ TEASPOON GROUND GINGER
½ TEASPOON DRY MUSTARD
½ TEASPOON SUGAR
1 POUND FLANK STEAK

1. Preheat the broiler or prepare the grill. If broiling, line a broiler pan with foil and lightly oil the rack. If grilling, lightly oil the grill rack.

2. In a small bowl, mix the pepper, onion powder, garlic powder, paprika, salt, Worcestershire sauce, ginger, mustard, and sugar.

3. Pat the steak dry. Rub the spice mixture over both sides of the steak. Place the steak on the prepared broiler pan or grill.

4. Broil or grill the steak 4 to 6 inches from the heat 5 minutes per side for medium-rare meat. Transfer the steak to a cutting board and let rest for 5 minutes. Thinly slice the steak across the grain and on the diagonal and serve.

KITCHEN NOTE: *This spice rub mixture is great to have on hand. Make four times the recipe at one time and store it in an airtight container in a cool, dry place up to 2 months. Rub it on beef, pork, or poultry before grilling.*

Pork Chops with Tangy Barbecue Sauce

1 TABLESPOON VEGETABLE OIL

1 SMALL ONION, FINELY CHOPPED

2 TEASPOONS CHILI POWDER

½ CUP FRESH ORANGE JUICE

⅓ CUP KETCHUP

1 TABLESPOON BROWN SUGAR

¼ TEASPOON GROUND GINGER

4 LOIN PORK CHOPS (¾ INCH THICK, ABOUT 1¾ POUNDS TOTAL)

¼ TEASPOON SALT

¼ TEASPOON BLACK PEPPER

1. In a medium saucepan, warm the oil over medium heat. Add the onion and sauté until softened, about 5 minutes. Add the chili powder and cook, stirring frequently, for 1 minute. Add the orange juice and bring to a boil over medium-high heat. Boil for 2 minutes. Stir in the ketchup, brown sugar, and ginger and cook over medium heat, stirring occasionally, until heated through, about 2 minutes.

2. Preheat the broiler. Line a broiler pan with foil and lightly oil the rack.

3. Season the pork chops on both sides with salt and pepper and arrange on the prepared broiler pan. Spread a thin layer of sauce over the top and broil 4 inches from the heat for 4 minutes. Turn the pork chops over and spread with more sauce. Broil for 4 minutes, or until just cooked through.

4. Serve the pork chops with any remaining barbecue sauce on the side.

Pork Broiler Dinner

SERVES 4

♡ LOW-FAT

¾ POUND PORK TENDERLOIN

¼ CUP BOTTLED FAT-FREE BARBECUE
  SAUCE

1 LARGE ONION, HALVED LENGTHWISE,
  THEN SLICED

2 SMALL YELLOW SQUASH, CUT IN
  HALF LENGTHWISE

2 TEASPOONS VEGETABLE OIL

½ TEASPOON SALT

1. Preheat the broiler. Line a broiler pan with foil and lightly oil the rack.

2. Place the pork in the center of the rack and brush with 2 tablespoons of the barbecue sauce. Arrange the onion on one side of the pork and the squash halves, cut side up, down the other side. Brush the vegetables with the oil and sprinkle with the salt.

3. Broil 4 to 6 inches from the heat for 8 minutes. Turn the pork and brush with the remaining barbecue sauce. Broil for 4 to 6 minutes, or until the meat is just barely pink in the center, and the vegetables are tender.

4. Transfer the pork to a cutting board and let rest for 5 minutes. Cut the pork into thin slices and arrange on serving plates with the onion and squash.

VARIATION: *This easy meal-in-one can also be made with skinless, boneless chicken breast halves. Lightly pound the chicken to even thickness and broil, brushing with the barbecue sauce, for about 5 minutes per side.*

Southern Barbecued Ham Steaks

SERVES 4

½ cup apricot preserves

⅓ cup fresh lemon juice

1 teaspoon minced fresh ginger

1 teaspoon Dijon mustard

1½ pounds ham steaks

1. Preheat the broiler or prepare the grill. If broiling, line a broiler pan with foil and lightly oil the rack. If grilling, lightly oil the grill rack.

2. In a small saucepan, warm the preserves, lemon juice, ginger, and mustard over medium-low heat, stirring until the preserves are melted and the mixture is smooth, 2 to 3 minutes.

3. Put the ham steaks on the prepared broiler pan or grill. Brush the top with some of the sauce.

4. Grill or broil the ham steaks 4 to 6 inches from the heat, turning once and brushing with more sauce, until golden brown, about 10 minutes. Serve right away.

Variation: *Try pineapple or peach preserves in place of apricot. Whichever you choose, this easy glaze is also good on chicken or pork tenderloin.*

Grilled Sausages and Peppers

SERVES 4

4 SWEET OR HOT ITALIAN SAUSAGE
   LINKS
¼ CUP OLIVE OIL
1½ TEASPOONS MINCED FRESH
   ROSEMARY, OR ½ TEASPOON DRIED,
   CRUMBLED

4 MEDIUM CUBANELLE PEPPERS OR
   ANAHEIM CHILI PEPPERS,
   QUARTERED LENGTHWISE
4 PLUM TOMATOES, CUT IN HALF
   LENGTHWISE
4 GRINDER OR HERO ROLLS, SPLIT

I. Prepare the grill or preheat the broiler. If broiling, line a broiler pan with foil.

2. Cut the sausages almost in half lengthwise so that they will lie flat. Set aside.

3. In a small bowl, combine the olive oil and rosemary. Brush the peppers and tomatoes with some of the oil mixture.

4. Arrange the sausages and vegetables on the prepared broiler pan or grill. Grill or broil the vegetables 4 inches from the heat, turning often, until they have softened and the skins are lightly charred, about 10 minutes. Grill or broil the sausages until browned and cooked through, 5 to 7 minutes.

5. Meanwhile, grill or toast the rolls, brushing the cut sides with more of the oil mixture.

6. Set the sausages on the rolls, top each with the grilled peppers and tomatoes, and drizzle with any remaining oil.

Substitution: *Cubanelle peppers, also referred to as frying peppers, are elongated, tapered sweet peppers that are pale green in color. Anaheim chilies are elongated dark green peppers with a very mild flavor. Both of these peppers are available in most large supermarkets; however, green bell peppers can also be used.*

MAPLE-GLAZED LAMB CHOPS

SERVES 4

¼ CUP PURE MAPLE SYRUP

¼ CUP COARSE-GRAIN MUSTARD

1½ TEASPOONS CIDER VINEGAR

¼ TEASPOON DRIED THYME

⅛ TEASPOON BLACK PEPPER

8 LOIN OR RIB LAMB CHOPS (1 INCH THICK, 2½ POUNDS TOTAL)

1. Preheat the broiler or prepare the grill. If broiling, line a broiler pan with foil.

2. In a small bowl, combine the maple syrup, mustard, vinegar, thyme, and pepper.

3. Arrange the lamb chops on the prepared broiler pan or grill. Broil or grill 4 to 6 inches from the heat, brushing frequently with the glaze and turning once, until the lamb chops are browned on the outside but still pink on the inside, 8 to 10 minutes. Serve right away.

KITCHEN NOTE: *For a hearty meal, serve these delectable chops with puréed butternut squash, steamed green beans, and warm buttermilk biscuits.*

Lamb with Tomato-Mint Salsa

SERVES 4

3 PLUM TOMATOES, SEEDED AND
    CHOPPED
2 TABLESPOONS OLIVE OIL
1 GARLIC CLOVE, MINCED
2 TABLESPOONS FINELY CHOPPED
    SCALLIONS
1 TABLESPOON FINELY CHOPPED FRESH
    MINT

1 TEASPOON RED WINE VINEGAR
½ TEASPOON SALT
4 CENTER-CUT LAMB STEAKS OR
    SHOULDER CHOPS (½ INCH THICK,
    ABOUT 1½ POUNDS TOTAL)
¼ TEASPOON BLACK PEPPER

1. Preheat the broiler or prepare the grill. If broiling, line a broiler pan with foil.

2. In a small nonreactive bowl, combine the tomatoes, 1 tablespoon of the olive oil, the garlic, scallions, mint, vinegar, and ¼ teaspoon of salt. Set aside.

3. Brush the lamb steaks with the remaining 1 tablespoon of oil and sprinkle both sides with the remaining ¼ teaspoon of salt and the pepper.

4. Arrange the lamb on the prepared broiler pan or the grill. Grill or broil 4 to 6 inches from the heat for 3 to 4 minutes per side for medium-rare meat.

5. Transfer the lamb steaks to serving plates and top each with some of the salsa.

Tropical Chicken Kebabs with Hoisin Glaze

SERVES 4

♡ LOW-FAT

¼ CUP HOISIN SAUCE

3 TABLESPOONS ORANGE JUICE

1 TABLESPOON SOY SAUCE

2 TEASPOONS MINCED FRESH GINGER

2 TEASPOONS CIDER VINEGAR

1½ POUNDS SKINLESS, BONELESS CHICKEN BREASTS, CUT INTO 1-INCH PIECES

ONE 20-OUNCE CAN JUICE-PACKED PINEAPPLE CHUNKS, DRAINED

1 MEDIUM GREEN BELL PEPPER, CUT INTO 1-INCH SQUARES

1 MEDIUM RED BELL PEPPER, CUT INTO 1-INCH SQUARES

1. Prepare the grill or preheat the broiler. If broiling, line a rimmed baking sheet with foil.

2. In a small bowl, blend the hoisin sauce, orange juice, soy sauce, ginger, and vinegar. Set aside.

3. Dividing the ingredients evenly, thread the chicken pieces (fold large pieces over to double), pineapple chunks, and bell pepper squares alternately on 8 to 12 skewers. Brush the kebabs with the sauce. If broiling, place the kebabs on the prepared baking sheet before brushing them.

4. Grill or broil the kebabs 4 to 6 inches from the heat for 2 to 3 minutes, or until the chicken begins to brown. Turn the kebabs, brush them with the sauce, and broil or grill for 2 to 3 minutes, or just until the chicken is cooked through.

KITCHEN NOTE: *If you are using bamboo skewers, first soak them in water for at least 30 minutes to prevent them from burning when placed on the grill or under the broiler.*

Lemon-Honey Chicken Breasts

SERVES 4

♡ LOW-FAT

3 TABLESPOONS FRESH LEMON JUICE

1 TABLESPOON HONEY

1 TABLESPOON VEGETABLE OIL

1 TEASPOON SOY SAUCE

¼ TEASPOON GROUND GINGER

4 SKINLESS, BONELESS CHICKEN BREAST HALVES (ABOUT 1¼ POUNDS TOTAL)

1. In a shallow dish, combine the lemon juice, honey, oil, soy sauce, and ginger. Add the chicken breasts, turn to coat, and let stand for 10 minutes.

2. Meanwhile, preheat the broiler or prepare the grill. If broiling, line a broiler pan with foil and lightly oil the rack. If grilling, lightly oil the grill rack.

3. Remove the chicken from the marinade, reserving the marinade. Arrange the chicken on the prepared broiler pan or grill.

4. Broil or grill the chicken breasts 4 to 6 inches from the heat for 6 to 8 minutes per side, brushing with the reserved marinade, or until golden brown and just cooked through.

KITCHEN NOTE: *Sprinkling dried herbs such as oregano, thyme, or rosemary over the hot coals just before grilling will impart a slight flavor and fragrance to the grilled foods.*

Broiled Herbed Chicken Thighs

SERVES 4

3 TABLESPOONS FRESH LEMON JUICE
1½ TABLESPOONS UNSALTED BUTTER,
MELTED
1½ TABLESPOONS OLIVE OIL
1 TABLESPOON WORCESTERSHIRE
SAUCE

½ TEASPOON DRIED BASIL
½ TEASPOON DRIED OREGANO
¼ TEASPOON DRIED THYME
8 SMALL SKINLESS, BONE-IN CHICKEN
THIGHS (ABOUT 1¾ POUNDS TOTAL)

1. Preheat the broiler.

2. In a shallow baking dish large enough to hold the chicken thighs in a single layer, combine the lemon juice, butter, oil, Worcestershire sauce, and herbs. Add the chicken and turn to coat.

3. Broil the chicken thighs, bone side down, 4 to 6 inches from the heat for 6 minutes.

Turn them over, brush with some of the herb mixture, and broil for 6 minutes. Turn them over again, brush with more of the herb mixture, and broil for 6 to 8 minutes, or until the juices run clear when the meat is pierced with the tip of a knife near the bone.

4. Transfer the chicken thighs to serving plates and spoon any remaining pan juices

KITCHEN NOTE: *To release more flavor from dried herbs, crumble them between your fingers before adding them to a mixture. If substituting dried herbs for fresh, use a 3-to-1 ratio. For every 1 tablespoon of fresh use 1 teaspoon dried, and vice versa.*

Tandoori Chicken with Cucumber Raita

 LOW - FAT

1 TEASPOON GROUND CUMIN

¼ TEASPOON CAYENNE PEPPER

¼ TEASPOON GROUND CINNAMON

¼ TEASPOON GROUND CLOVES

¼ TEASPOON GROUND GINGER

¼ TEASPOON SALT

4 SKINLESS, BONELESS CHICKEN BREAST HALVES (1¼ POUNDS TOTAL), POUNDED TO ½ INCH THICK

2 TEASPOONS VEGETABLE OIL

1 CUP PLAIN LOW-FAT YOGURT

¾ CUP FINELY CHOPPED, PEELED AND SEEDED CUCUMBER

2 TABLESPOONS CHOPPED FRESH MINT

1. Preheat the broiler or prepare the grill. If broiling, line a broiler pan with foil and lightly oil the rack. If grilling, lightly oil the grill rack.

2. In a small bowl, mix the cumin, cayenne, cinnamon, cloves, ginger, and salt. Brush both sides of the chicken breasts with the oil, then rub the spice mixture onto both sides of each breast.

3. In a small bowl, combine the yogurt, cucumber, and mint. Set aside.

4. Arrange the chicken on the prepared broiler pan or grill. Broil or grill 4 to 6 inches from the heat for 5 to 6 minutes per side, or just until cooked through.

5. Serve the chicken with the cucumber raita on the side.

KITCHEN NOTE: *Raita is a cool and refreshing yogurt-based relish popular in India, where it is a balance to spicy dishes. Many different combinations of chopped vegetables and herbs may be added to the yogurt, but cucumber and mint are the most popular.*

Mexican Turkey Burgers

SERVES 4

1 POUND GROUND TURKEY

1 TABLESPOON OLIVE OIL

1½ TEASPOONS GROUND CUMIN

1 CUP BOTTLED SALSA, DRAINED

4 SLICES MONTEREY JACK CHEESE
(OPTIONAL)

4 KAISER ROLLS, SPLIT

FOR TOPPING: ADDITIONAL SALSA AND
CHOPPED AVOCADO (OPTIONAL)

1. Prepare the grill or preheat the broiler. If broiling, line a broiler pan with foil and lightly oil the rack. If grilling, lightly oil the grill rack.

2. In a medium bowl, combine the turkey, oil, cumin, and salsa. Form the mixture into four ½-inch-thick patties.

3. Arrange the burgers on the prepared broiler pan or grill.

4. Broil or grill the burgers 4 to 6 inches from the heat for 3 to 4 minutes per side, or just until cooked through. Add the cheese for the last 3 minutes, if desired.

5. Meanwhile, grill or toast the kaiser rolls.

6. Set the burgers on the buns and top each one with additional salsa and chopped avocado, if desired.

VARIATION: *This spicy ground turkey mixture also makes delicious tacos. In a large skillet, warm 1 tablespoon of vegetable oil over medium-high heat. Mix the turkey, cumin, and drained salsa. Add to the skillet and cook until the turkey is browned, about 10 minutes. Serve in taco shells with shredded lettuce, diced tomatoes, and sour cream.*

Grilled Turkey in Pitas with Peanut Sauce

SERVES 4

♡ LOW-FAT

FOUR 7-INCH WHOLE-WHEAT PITA
    BREADS
2 TABLESPOONS CREAMY PEANUT
    BUTTER
1 TABLESPOON SOY SAUCE
1 TABLESPOON ORIENTAL (DARK)
    SESAME OIL
2 TEASPOONS FRESH LEMON JUICE

1 TEASPOON SUGAR
½ TEASPOON MINCED GARLIC
4 THIN-SLICED TURKEY BREAST
    CUTLETS (ABOUT 1 POUND TOTAL)
1 MEDIUM GRANNY SMITH APPLE,
    THINLY SLICED
1 CUP PACKED WATERCRESS SPRIGS

1. Preheat the broiler or prepare the grill. If broiling, line a broiler pan with foil and lightly oil the rack. If grilling, lightly oil the grill rack.

2. Wrap the pitas in foil and warm them on the grill or in the oven for 5 to 10 minutes.

3. Meanwhile, in a small bowl, combine the peanut butter, soy sauce, sesame oil, 1 tablespoon water, lemon juice, sugar, and garlic. Set aside.

4. Arrange the turkey cutlets on the prepared broiler pan or grill.

5. Broil or grill the turkey cutlets 4 to 6 inches from the heat for about 2 minutes per side, or just until cooked through.

6. Slice a sliver off the top edge of each pita and partially split them. Tuck a turkey cutlet into each pita. Spoon in about 1 tablespoon of the peanut sauce, then fill with the apple slices and watercress sprigs.

VARIATION: *These sandwiches can also be made using pork loin cutlets, or you can purchase a 1-pound piece of lean boneless pork loin and cut it into 8 thin slices, then pound them very thin. Use 2 pork cutlets for each sandwich.*

Fresh Salmon Burgers

SERVES 4

1 POUND BONELESS, SKINLESS SALMON
   FILLET, WELL CHOPPED
¼ CUP REDUCED-FAT MAYONNAISE
2 TABLESPOONS UNSEASONED DRY
   BREAD CRUMBS
1 TABLESPOON DIJON MUSTARD
1 TABLESPOON MINCED ONION
2 TEASPOONS FRESH LEMON JUICE

½ TEASPOON MINCED GARLIC
½ TEASPOON SALT
½ TEASPOON BLACK PEPPER
4 SOURDOUGH SANDWICH ROLLS
2 TABLESPOONS UNSALTED BUTTER, AT
   ROOM TEMPERATURE
¼ CUP BOTTLED TARTAR SAUCE

1. Prepare the grill or preheat the broiler. If broiling, line a broiler pan with foil and lightly oil the rack. If grilling, lightly oil the grill rack.

2. In a medium bowl, combine the salmon, mayonnaise, bread crumbs, mustard, onion, lemon juice, garlic, salt, and pepper. Form the salmon mixture into 4 patties, about ¾ inch thick.

3. Arrange the burgers on the prepared broiler pan or grill.

4. Grill or broil the burgers 4 inches from the heat for 3 to 4 minutes per side, or just until cooked through.

5. Meanwhile, grill or toast the rolls. Brush the cut sides with the softened butter.

6. Set the burgers on the buns and top each one with a spoonful of tartar sauce.

GRILLED SESAME SHRIMP SKEWERS

SERVES 4

♡ LOW-FAT

1 POUND UNCOOKED LARGE SHRIMP
(ABOUT 20)
1½ TABLESPOONS SOY SAUCE
1 TABLESPOON FRESH LEMON JUICE
1 TEASPOON ORIENTAL (DARK) SESAME
OIL

½ TEASPOON MINCED FRESH GINGER
½ TEASPOON GROUND CUMIN
2 TEASPOONS SESAME SEEDS

1. Preheat the broiler or prepare the grill. If broiling, line a rimmed baking sheet with foil.

2. Thread the shrimp onto 4 to 8 skewers, pushing the skewer through both the head and tail end of each shrimp.

3. In a small bowl, combine the soy sauce, lemon juice, oil, ginger, and cumin. Brush the

soy mixture over both sides of the shrimp skewers, then sprinkle with sesame seeds. If broiling, place the skewers on the prepared baking sheet before brushing them.

4. Grill or broil the skewers 4 inches from the heat until the shrimp are opaque in the center, 3 to 4 minutes per side.

VARIATION: *The best thing about kebab recipes is their versatility. These skewers can also be made with 1 pound of sea scallops, at least ¾ inch in diameter, or 2-inch chunks of fresh swordfish, salmon, or tuna.*

Swordfish with Fresh Tomato Salad

SERVES 4

2 POUNDS ASSORTED TOMATOES (SUCH AS CHERRY, BEEFSTEAK, AND YELLOW PLUM TOMATOES)
3 TABLESPOONS BALSAMIC VINEGAR
3 TABLESPOONS OLIVE OIL
2 GARLIC CLOVES, MINCED
3 TABLESPOONS CHOPPED FRESH BASIL, OR ½ TEASPOON DRIED
½ TEASPOON SALT
¼ TEASPOON BLACK PEPPER
4 SWORDFISH STEAKS (ABOUT 6 OUNCES EACH)

1. Halve the small tomatoes and cut the larger ones into 1-inch chunks. In a medium bowl, combine the tomatoes, vinegar, olive oil, garlic, basil, salt, and pepper. Let stand at room temperature while you grill the fish.

2. Preheat the broiler or prepare the grill. If broiling, line a broiler pan with foil and lightly oil the rack. If grilling, lightly oil the grill rack.

3. Arrange the fish on the prepared broiler pan or grill. Grill or broil the fish 4 inches from the heat for 3 to 4 minutes on each side, or until the fish flakes easily with a fork.

4. Transfer the fish to serving plates. Divide the tomato mixture over each serving and serve right away.

SKILLET DISHES AND STIR-FRIES

GARLICKY MEATBALL SKILLET

SERVES 4

1 POUND LEAN GROUND BEEF

1 LARGE EGG

¼ CUP SEASONED DRY BREAD CRUMBS

3 TABLESPOONS GRATED PARMESAN
CHEESE

¼ TEASPOON SALT

¼ TEASPOON BLACK PEPPER

ONE 10-OUNCE PACKAGE FROZEN CUT
GREEN BEANS, THAWED

ONE 15-OUNCE CAN SMALL WHITE
POTATOES, DRAINED AND
QUARTERED

ONE 14½-OUNCE CAN STEWED
TOMATOES

4 GARLIC CLOVES, MINCED

1. In a medium bowl, mix the beef, egg, bread crumbs, cheese, salt, and pepper. Form the mixture into 16 meatballs.

2. In a large, deep nonstick skillet, brown the meatballs over medium-high heat, turning occasionally, for 3 minutes.

3. Add the green beans, potatoes, tomatoes, and garlic. Bring to a boil over medium-high heat. Reduce the heat to medium-low, cover, and simmer for 8 minutes, stirring occasionally, until the green beans are tender and the meatballs are cooked through.

Pan-Fried Cube Steaks with Onions and Peppers

SERVES 4

¼ CUP FLOUR

¼ TEASPOON SALT

½ TEASPOON BLACK PEPPER

1 POUND CUBE STEAKS, CUT INTO 4 PIECES

2 TABLESPOONS VEGETABLE OIL

1 LARGE ONION, THINLY SLICED

1 LARGE RED BELL PEPPER, CUT INTO THIN STRIPS

1 LARGE GREEN BELL PEPPER, CUT INTO THIN STRIPS

ONE 14½-OUNCE CAN STEWED TOMATOES

½ CUP BEEF BROTH, PREFERABLY REDUCED-SODIUM

1 TEASPOON DRIED OREGANO

1. On a sheet of wax paper, combine the flour, salt, and pepper. Dredge the cube steaks in the flour mixture and shake off the excess. Reserve the flour mixture.

2. In a large skillet, warm 1 tablespoon of the oil over medium-high heat. Add the cube steaks and cook until browned, about 2 minutes per side. Transfer the steaks to a plate.

3. Warm the remaining tablespoon of oil in the skillet over medium heat. Add the onion and bell peppers and sauté until the vegetables just begin to soften, about 5 minutes.

4. Stir in the reserved flour mixture until no longer visible. Add the tomatoes, beef broth, and oregano. Return the steaks to the skillet with any extracted juices.

5. Reduce the heat to medium-low, cover, and simmer until the steaks are tender, about 5 minutes. Uncover and simmer for 2 minutes, until the sauce is slightly thickened.

KITCHEN NOTE: *Cube steaks are thin cuts of beef round that are put through a tenderizing machine, leaving crisscross marks on the meat. These steaks are also good for quick steak sandwiches.*

Ginger Beef Stir-Fry

SERVES 4

2 TABLESPOONS SOY SAUCE

2 TEASPOONS ORIENTAL (DARK) SESAME OIL

1 TABLESPOON MINCED GARLIC

1 TABLESPOON MINCED FRESH GINGER

1½ TEASPOONS SUGAR

½ TEASPOON CRUSHED RED PEPPER FLAKES

1 POUND STIR-FRY BEEF ROUND STRIPS, CUT IN HALF CROSSWISE

½ CUP BEEF BROTH, PREFERABLY REDUCED-SODIUM

1 TABLESPOON CORNSTARCH

1 LARGE RED BELL PEPPER

2 TABLESPOONS VEGETABLE OIL

2 CUPS BROCCOLI FLORETS

1. In a medium bowl, combine 1 tablespoon of the soy sauce, 1 teaspoon of the sesame oil, the garlic, ginger, sugar, and red pepper flakes. Stir in the beef. Set aside.

2. In a small bowl, blend the beef broth, the remaining soy sauce, and the cornstarch. Set aside. Cut the bell pepper into thin strips and set aside.

3. In a large heavy skillet or wok, warm 1 tablespoon of the oil over high heat. Add the beef mixture and stir-fry until the meat is browned, 1 to 2 minutes. Transfer the beef to a plate.

4. Add the remaining 1 tablespoon of oil to the skillet and warm over high heat. Add the broccoli and bell pepper strips and stir-fry until crisp-tender, about 3 minutes.

5. Return the beef to the skillet. Stir the broth mixture, add it to the skillet, and bring the liquid to a boil. Cook, stirring frequently, until the vegetables are tender, the beef is cooked through, and the sauce has thickened, 1 to 2 minutes.

6. Drizzle with the remaining 1 teaspoon sesame oil and serve hot.

KITCHEN NOTE: *The availability of packaged, precut strips of meat and poultry makes stir-fry dishes easy to prepare. Look for beef stir-fry packages in the meat section of large supermarkets. If they are unavailable, purchase 1 pound of boneless beef sirloin and cut it across the grain into 2 x ⅛-inch diagonal strips. This recipe will work with stir-fry chicken tenderloin strips as well; just replace the beef broth with chicken broth.*

Hungarian Beef and Noodles

SERVES 4

1 POUND LEAN GROUND BEEF

1 MEDIUM ONION, CHOPPED

1 MEDIUM GREEN BELL PEPPER, CHOPPED

1 GARLIC CLOVE, MINCED

1 TABLESPOON PAPRIKA

1 TEASPOON DRIED THYME

3½ CUPS BEEF BROTH, PREFERABLY REDUCED-SODIUM

4 CUPS MEDIUM-WIDTH EGG NOODLES

ONE 10-OUNCE PACKAGE FROZEN PEAS AND CARROTS

¼ CUP SOUR CREAM

1. In a large nonstick skillet, brown the beef over medium-high heat, breaking up any large chunks with a spoon.

2. Stir in the onion, bell pepper, and garlic and cook, stirring often, for 5 minutes. Stir in the paprika and thyme.

3. Add the broth, noodles, and peas and carrots. Bring to a boil over medium-high heat. Reduce the heat to low, cover, and simmer for 8 to 10 minutes, stirring occasionally, until the noodles are tender.

4. Stir the sour cream into the noodle mixture and simmer, uncovered, for 2 minutes. Serve hot.

Beef Tenderloin with Red Wine-Mushroom Sauce

SERVES 4

4 BEEF TENDERLOIN STEAKS (ABOUT
   1¼ POUNDS TOTAL)
1½ TEASPOONS COARSELY GROUND
   BLACK PEPPER
1 TABLESPOON UNSALTED BUTTER
1½ TEASPOONS VEGETABLE OIL
¼ CUP MINCED SHALLOTS

1 GARLIC CLOVE, MINCED
½ CUP DRY RED WINE OR BEEF BROTH,
   PREFERABLY REDUCED-SODIUM
2 CUPS THINLY SLICED MUSHROOMS
¾ CUP HEAVY CREAM
¼ TEASPOON SALT
⅛ TEASPOON BLACK PEPPER

1. Pat the steaks dry. Rub the pepper onto both sides of each steak.

2. In a large heavy skillet, warm ½ tablespoon of the butter and the oil over medium-high heat. Add the steaks and cook until browned, about 2 minutes per side. Reduce the heat to medium and cook, turning occasionally, for about 6 minutes for rare meat, or 7 to 8 minutes for medium-rare. Transfer the steaks to warmed plates and loosely cover with foil to keep warm.

3. Pour off the drippings and warm the remaining ½ tablespoon of butter in the skillet over medium heat until melted. Add the shallots and garlic and sauté for 1 minute.

4. Add the wine to the skillet and bring to a boil over high heat, stirring to scrape up any browned bits. Boil for 1 minute.

5. Add the mushrooms and cook, stirring frequently, until softened, about 3 minutes. Add the cream and simmer until the mixture begins to thicken, about 1 minute. Season with the salt and pepper.

6. Spoon the sauce over the steaks and serve.

Kitchen Note: *This recipe also makes a wonderfully easy and elegant meal to serve to guests. Just accompany it with roasted new potatoes and a steamed green vegetable such as asparagus or green beans.*

GREEK LAMB STIR-FRY

SERVES 4

1 POUND LEAN GROUND LAMB

2 GARLIC CLOVES, MINCED

1 TEASPOON DRIED OREGANO, CRUMBLED

½ CUP CHICKEN BROTH

3 TABLESPOONS SOY SAUCE

3 TABLESPOONS TOMATO PASTE

3 TABLESPOONS OLIVE OIL

1 SMALL UNPEELED EGGPLANT, CUT INTO 1-INCH CUBES (2 CUPS)

1 LARGE RED OR YELLOW BELL PEPPER, CUT INTO 1-INCH SQUARES

¼ CUP CHOPPED FRESH MINT

2 OUNCES FETA CHEESE, CRUMBLED (½ CUP)

1. In a medium bowl, mix the lamb, garlic, and oregano. Set aside.

2. In a small bowl, mix the broth, soy sauce, and tomato paste. Set aside.

3. In a large skillet or wok, warm 1 tablespoon of the oil over medium-high heat. Add the lamb mixture and stir-fry, breaking up the meat with a large spoon, until browned, about 3 minutes. Transfer the lamb to a large bowl.

4. Pour off the drippings and warm the remaining 2 tablespoons of oil in the skillet over medium-high heat. Add the eggplant and stir-fry until softened slightly, about 3 minutes. Add the bell pepper and stir-fry until crisp-tender and the eggplant is tender, about 2 minutes. Transfer the vegetables to the bowl with the lamb.

5. Stir the broth mixture, add it to the skillet, and bring to a boil over high heat. Boil for 30 seconds, or until thickened slightly.

6. Return the lamb and vegetables to the skillet and stir to coat with the sauce. Stir in the mint. Sprinkle with the cheese and serve hot.

SUBSTITUTION: *This flavorful stir-fry is also very tasty when made with ground beef.*

PORK CHOPS PROVENÇALE

SERVES 4

1 TABLESPOON VEGETABLE OIL

1 TABLESPOON UNSALTED BUTTER

4 LOIN PORK CHOPS, WITH BONE
(ABOUT 2 POUNDS TOTAL)

½ CUP CHICKEN BROTH, PREFERABLY
REDUCED-SODIUM

¼ CUP WHITE WINE, OR ADDITIONAL
BROTH

1 GARLIC CLOVE, MINCED

1 TEASPOON CORNSTARCH

1 TEASPOON DIJON MUSTARD

1 TEASPOON DRIED SAGE

⅓ CUP SLICED PIMIENTO-STUFFED
GREEN OLIVES

¼ TEASPOON SALT

¼ TEASPOON BLACK PEPPER

1. In a large skillet, warm the oil and butter over medium-high heat. Add the pork chops and cook until browned, about 6 minutes per side.

2. Meanwhile, in a glass measuring cup, combine the broth, wine, garlic, cornstarch, mustard, and sage.

3. Transfer the pork chops to a plate and cover loosely with foil to keep warm.

4. Stir the broth mixture and pour it into the skillet, stirring to scrape up any browned bits. Bring to a boil over high heat and boil until thickened slightly, about 1 minute. Stir in the olives, salt, and pepper.

5. Transfer the pork chops to serving plates and spoon the sauce over them.

SUBSTITUTION: *The garlic, olives, and herbs earn this dish the title Provençale, after the Provence region of France where these are widely used. The recipe is equally good when skinless, boneless chicken breast halves are used in place of the pork chops.*

Pork Cutlets with Sautéed Apples

SERVES 4

⅓ CUP UNSEASONED DRY BREAD
   CRUMBS
8 THIN PORK CUTLETS (ABOUT
   1 POUND TOTAL)
3 TABLESPOONS DIJON MUSTARD

2 TABLESPOONS VEGETABLE OIL
3 TABLESPOONS UNSALTED BUTTER
2 GRANNY SMITH APPLES, PEELED AND
   CUT INTO THIN SLICES
2 TABLESPOONS SUGAR

1. Spread the bread crumbs onto a sheet of wax paper. Brush the pork cutlets on both sides with the mustard, then coat with the bread crumbs.

2. In a large skillet, warm the oil over medium-high heat. Add the pork and cook until browned, about 2 minutes on each side. Transfer the pork to a serving platter and cover with foil.

3. Add the butter to the skillet and warm over medium heat until melted. Add the apples and sauté until softened, about 3 minutes. Add the sugar, stirring to scrape any loose bits from pan. Cook until the sugar has dissolved and the apples are tender, about 2 minutes.

4. Spoon the apples over the pork cutlets and serve.

Sautéed Rosemary Pork Medallions

SERVES 4

¼ CUP FLOUR
¼ TEASPOON SALT
¼ TEASPOON BLACK PEPPER
1 POUND PORK TENDERLOIN, CUT
    DIAGONALLY INTO 8 SLICES
2 TABLESPOONS OLIVE OIL
½ CUP DRY WHITE WINE

¼ CUP MINCED SHALLOTS
1 GARLIC CLOVE, MINCED
1 CUP CHICKEN BROTH, PREFERABLY
    REDUCED-SODIUM
1 TABLESPOON CHOPPED FRESH
    ROSEMARY, OR 1 TEASPOON DRIED
1 TABLESPOON UNSALTED BUTTER

1. On a sheet of wax paper, mix the flour, salt, and pepper. Dredge the pork slices in the flour mixture and shake off the excess.

2. In a large skillet, warm the oil over medium heat. Add the pork slices and cook until just barely pink in center, about 3 minutes per side. Transfer the pork to a serving platter and cover loosely with foil to keep warm.

3. Wipe out the skillet. Add the wine, shallots, and garlic, and bring to a boil over medium-high heat. Boil until the wine is reduced to about 2 tablespoons, 2 to 3 minutes.

4. Add the chicken broth and bring to a boil. Boil until the liquid is reduced to about ½ cup, 2 to 3 minutes.

5. Remove the skillet from the heat. Stir in the rosemary and butter. Pour the sauce over the pork slices and serve.

Knockwurst and Hot Cabbage Salad

SERVES 4

2 TABLESPOONS VEGETABLE OIL

1 MEDIUM ONION, CHOPPED

3 TABLESPOONS CIDER VINEGAR

2 TABLESPOONS BROWN SUGAR

¼ TEASPOON SALT

½ TEASPOON BLACK PEPPER

5 CUPS SHREDDED RED CABBAGE

1 MEDIUM GRANNY SMITH APPLE,
    THINLY SLICED

¾ POUND FULLY COOKED KNOCKWURST,
    CUT INTO ½-INCH-THICK SLICES

1. In a large skillet, warm the oil over medium heat. Add the onion and sauté until softened, about 5 minutes. Stir in the vinegar, sugar, salt, and pepper.

2. Add the cabbage and apple and stir well to combine. Bring the mixture to a boil over medium-high heat.

3. Arrange the sausage slices over the cabbage mixture. Reduce the heat to medium-low, cover, and simmer until the cabbage is tender, about 10 minutes. Serve hot.

SWEET AFTERTHOUGHT: *What would be better after a German-style dinner than a slice of warm gingerbread? Prepare a packaged mix, bake it while you eat, and serve it warm, topped with whipped cream or nondairy topping.*

Ham and Mushroom Hash

SERVES 4

2 TABLESPOONS OLIVE OIL

4 MEDIUM UNPEELED RED POTATOES,
CUT INTO 1-INCH CHUNKS

3 GARLIC CLOVES, MINCED

¾ POUND MUSHROOMS, QUARTERED

1½ CUPS CUBED HAM

1 TABLESPOON CHOPPED FRESH THYME,
OR 1 TEASPOON DRIED

1¾ CUPS CHICKEN BROTH, PREFERABLY
REDUCED-SODIUM

1½ TEASPOONS CORNSTARCH

2 TABLESPOONS CHOPPED FRESH
PARSLEY

¼ TEASPOON SALT

¼ TEASPOON BLACK PEPPER

1. In a large skillet, warm the oil over medium-high heat. Add the potatoes and sauté until lightly browned, about 5 minutes. Add the garlic and mushrooms and sauté until the mushrooms are softened, about 3 minutes. Stir in the ham and thyme.

2. Add the chicken broth and bring to a boil over medium-high heat. Reduce the heat to medium-low, cover, and simmer until the potatoes are cooked through, about 15 minutes.

3. In a small cup, blend the cornstarch and 1 tablespoon water. Add the cornstarch mixture to the skillet, stir well, and bring to a boil. Boil for 1 minute, until the sauce has thickened slightly. Stir in the parsley, salt, and pepper, and serve.

Simmered Chicken and Zucchini

SERVES 4

♡ LOW - FAT

2 TEASPOONS VEGETABLE OIL

1 TEASPOON CUMIN SEED

1 TEASPOON FENNEL SEED

1 MEDIUM ONION, THINLY SLICED

⅛ TEASPOON CAYENNE PEPPER

1 POUND SKINLESS, BONELESS CHICKEN
BREAST HALVES, CUT CROSSWISE
INTO ½-INCH-THICK STRIPS

2 MEDIUM ZUCCHINI, HALVED
LENGTHWISE AND THINLY SLICED
CROSSWISE

4 PLUM TOMATOES, CHOPPED

2 TABLESPOONS CHOPPED FRESH
PARSLEY

¼ TEASPOON SALT

⅛ TEASPOON BLACK PEPPER

I. In a large nonstick skillet, warm the oil over medium heat. Add the cumin and fennel seeds and sauté for 30 seconds, until popped and fragrant.

2. Add the onion and cayenne and sauté over medium-high heat until the onion is softened, about 3 minutes. Add the chicken and sauté until golden, about 3 minutes.

3. Stir in the zucchini and tomatoes. Reduce the heat to medium-low, cover, and simmer until the zucchini is tender, about 5 minutes. Stir in the parsley, salt, and pepper, and serve.

KITCHEN NOTE: *All poultry should be rinsed under cold running water and patted dry before using. The rinsing will cleanse the meat of bacteria and other contaminants picked up during handling and packaging. Keep rinsed, raw poultry thoroughly chilled until you need it.*

SPICY LEMON CHICKEN

SERVES 4

♡ LOW - FAT

1 TABLESPOON VEGETABLE OIL

1¼ POUNDS STIR-FRY CHICKEN
   TENDERLOINS, HALVED CROSSWISE

1 GARLIC CLOVE, MINCED

1 TABLESPOON MINCED FRESH GINGER

⅓ CUP CHICKEN BROTH, PREFERABLY
   REDUCED-SODIUM

3 TABLESPOONS FRESH LEMON JUICE

1 TEASPOON GRATED LEMON ZEST

1 TABLESPOON SOY SAUCE

2 TEASPOONS CORNSTARCH

2 TEASPOONS SUGAR

1. In a large heavy skillet or wok, warm the oil over medium-high heat. Add the chicken, garlic, and ginger, and stir-fry until the chicken is lightly golden, but still slightly pink in the center, 2 to 3 minutes.

2. Add the chicken broth, lemon juice, and lemon zest. Bring the mixture to a boil over high heat. Reduce the heat to medium and simmer, uncovered, until the chicken is cooked through, about 5 minutes.

3. Meanwhile, in a small bowl, combine the soy sauce, 1 tablespoon water, cornstarch, and sugar. Add the mixture to the skillet and bring to a boil over medium-high heat. Boil for 1 minute, or until the sauce has thickened. Serve hot.

KITCHEN NOTE: *Lemons will yield more juice if they are warm or at room temperature. To warm lemons, place in a bowl of warm water for 5 minutes or microwave on medium power for 1 minute.*

Sweet and Sour Chicken Stir-Fry

SERVES 4

♡ LOW-FAT

1 POUND STIR-FRY CHICKEN
    TENDERLOINS, HALVED CROSSWISE

2 TABLESPOONS PLUS 1 TEASPOON
    CORNSTARCH

4 QUARTER-SIZE SLICES FRESH GINGER

1 LARGE RED BELL PEPPER

¼ CUP ORANGE JUICE

¼ CUP CHICKEN BROTH

2 TABLESPOONS RICE WINE VINEGAR

1 TABLESPOON SOY SAUCE

2 TABLESPOONS VEGETABLE OIL

ONE 9-OUNCE PACKAGE FROZEN
    SUGAR-SNAP PEAS, THAWED

ONE 8-OUNCE CAN SLICED WATER
    CHESTNUTS, DRAINED

4 THIN LEMON SLICES

1. Pat the chicken dry. In a small bowl, toss the chicken with 2 tablespoons of the cornstarch to coat evenly. Set aside. Cut the ginger and bell pepper into thin strips and set aside.

2. In a glass measuring cup, blend the orange juice, chicken broth, vinegar, soy sauce, and remaining 1 teaspoon of cornstarch. Set aside.

3. In a large heavy skillet or wok, warm 1 tablespoon of the oil over high heat. Add the chicken and stir-fry until opaque but still slightly pink in the center, 2 to 3 minutes. Transfer the chicken to a plate and set aside.

4. Add the remaining 1 tablespoon of oil to the skillet and warm over medium-high heat. Add the ginger and stir-fry for 10 seconds. Add the bell pepper, peas, and water chestnuts, and stir-fry until crisp-tender, 2 to 3 minutes.

5. Return the chicken to the skillet and stir in the lemon slices. Stir the orange juice mixture, add it to the skillet, and bring to a boil over high heat. Boil for 1 minute, or until the chicken is cooked through and the liquid has thickened. Serve hot.

CREOLE CHICKEN DRUMSTICKS

SERVES 4

2 TEASPOONS VEGETABLE OIL

8 SMALL SKINLESS CHICKEN DRUMSTICKS (ABOUT 1¾ POUNDS TOTAL)

1 LARGE ONION, THINLY SLICED

1 LARGE GREEN BELL PEPPER, HALVED AND THINLY SLICED

1 CUP CHICKEN BROTH, PREFERABLY REDUCED-SODIUM

ONE 14½-OUNCE CAN STEWED TOMATOES

1 TEASPOON DRIED THYME

1 TEASPOON HOT PEPPER SAUCE, OR TO TASTE

1 TEASPOON WORCESTERSHIRE SAUCE

ONE 10-OUNCE PACKAGE FROZEN CUT OKRA, THAWED

1. In a large nonstick skillet, warm 1 teaspoon of the oil over medium-high heat. Add the chicken and cook until browned, about 3 minutes per side. Transfer the chicken to a plate.

2. Warm the remaining teaspoon of oil in the skillet over medium heat. Add the onion and bell pepper and sauté until just beginning to soften, about 3 minutes. Add the chicken broth, stirring to scrape up any browned bits.

3. Add the tomatoes, thyme, hot pepper sauce, Worcestershire sauce, and okra to the skillet and stir to combine. Return the chicken to the skillet.

4. Bring the mixture to a boil over medium-high heat. Reduce the heat to medium-low, cover, and simmer for 15 minutes, stirring once or twice, until the vegetables are tender and the chicken is cooked through.

KITCHEN NOTE: *Creole cooking is a blend of many ethnic cuisines (most notably Spanish, French, and African) that have mingled over the last 300 years in Louisiana. Specific ingredients, such as tomatoes, bell peppers, onions, celery, okra, and cayenne, give Creole cooking its distinct and characteristic flavor.*

Chicken Tetrazzini

SERVES 4

2 TABLESPOONS UNSALTED BUTTER

1 TABLESPOON OLIVE OIL

1 POUND SKINLESS, BONELESS CHICKEN
BREAST HALVES, CUT CROSSWISE
INTO ½-INCH-THICK STRIPS

¼ TEASPOON SALT

¼ TEASPOON BLACK PEPPER

¼ TEASPOON PAPRIKA

¼ CUP MINCED SHALLOTS

½ POUND MUSHROOMS, QUARTERED

3 TABLESPOONS FLOUR

1½ CUPS HALF-AND-HALF

1 TABLESPOON DRY SHERRY

¼ CUP GRATED PARMESAN CHEESE

1. In a large skillet, warm 1 tablespoon of the butter and the oil over medium-high heat. Add the chicken and sprinkle with the salt, pepper, and paprika. Sauté until the chicken is golden brown, about 5 minutes. Transfer the chicken to a plate and set aside.

2. Warm the remaining 1 tablespoon of butter in the skillet over medium heat until melted. Add the shallots and mushrooms and sauté until the mushrooms are softened, about 5 minutes.

3. Sprinkle the flour into the skillet and cook, stirring constantly, until no longer visible. Stir in the half-and-half and sherry. Bring the mixture to a simmer. Reduce the heat to low and cook, stirring frequently, until the sauce has thickened, about 3 minutes.

4. Return the chicken to the skillet and stir in the Parmesan cheese. Cook, stirring occasionally, until the chicken is cooked through, 2 to 3 minutes.

KITCHEN NOTE: *It is said that this dish is named after Luisa Tetrazzini, an Italian opera singer who enjoyed a casserole version of the dish before going on stage.*

CHICKEN WITH CHILIES

SERVES 6

¼ CUP FLOUR
½ TEASPOON CHILI POWDER
⅛ TEASPOON CAYENNE PEPPER
6 SKINLESS, BONELESS CHICKEN BREAST
   HALVES (1¾ POUNDS), POUNDED
   ½ INCH THICK
2 TEASPOONS VEGETABLE OIL
ONE 10-OUNCE CAN MILD ENCHILADA
   SAUCE

ONE 11-OUNCE VACUUM-PACKED CAN
   CORN KERNELS
ONE 4-OUNCE CAN WHOLE GREEN
   CHILIES, DRAINED
½ CUP SHREDDED MONTEREY JACK
   CHEESE

1. In a large plastic food bag, combine the flour, chili powder, and cayenne. Add the chicken and shake to coat lightly.

2. In a large nonstick skillet, warm the oil over medium-high heat. Add the chicken to the skillet and cook until golden brown, about 2 minutes per side. Transfer the chicken to a plate.

3. Add the enchilada sauce and corn to the skillet and bring to a simmer over medium-high heat.

4. Arrange the chicken breasts over the sauce. Slice each green chili in half lengthwise. Place one green chili slice over each chicken breast and top with 2 tablespoons of the cheese.

5. Cover the skillet, reduce the heat to medium, and simmer until the chicken is cooked through and the cheese is melted, 5 to 7 minutes. Serve hot.

Moroccan Chicken and Couscous

SERVES 4

1 TABLESPOON OLIVE OIL

1 POUND SKINLESS, BONELESS CHICKEN
BREAST HALVES, CUT INTO BITE-SIZE
PIECES

4 PLUM TOMATOES

1 GARLIC CLOVE

1¼ CUPS CHICKEN BROTH, PREFERABLY
REDUCED-SODIUM

ONE 7¾-OUNCE CAN CHICKPEAS,
DRAINED

¾ TEASPOON GROUND CUMIN

½ TEASPOON CURRY POWDER

1 CUP INSTANT COUSCOUS

½ CUP SLICED GREEN OLIVES WITH
PIMIENTOS

¼ CUP FRESH LEMON JUICE

½ TEASPOON SALT

1. In a large skillet, warm the oil over medium heat. Add the chicken and sauté until lightly golden, 6 to 7 minutes.

2. Meanwhile, coarsely chop the tomatoes and mince the garlic.

3. Add the garlic to the skillet and sauté for 30 seconds. Add the tomatoes and sauté for 1 minute. Add the chicken broth, chickpeas, cumin, and curry powder, and bring to a boil over medium-high heat.

4. Stir in the couscous. Cover the skillet and remove from the heat. Let stand until the liquid is absorbed, 5 minutes.

5. Fluff the couscous with a fork and stir in the olives, lemon juice, and salt. Serve hot.

VARIATION: *If you would like to prepare a low-fat version of this dish, just omit the chickpeas and olives.*

TURKEY CASHEW STIR-FRY

SERVES 4

♡ LOW-FAT

2 MEDIUM CARROTS

4 SCALLIONS

2 TABLESPOONS SOY SAUCE

1 TEASPOON HONEY

1 TEASPOON ORIENTAL (DARK)
    SESAME OIL

2 TABLESPOONS PEANUT OIL

⅓ CUP CASHEW NUTS

1 POUND TURKEY BREAST CUTLETS,
    CUT CROSSWISE INTO THIN STRIPS

ONE 9-OUNCE PACKAGE FROZEN CUT
    ASPARAGUS, THAWED

1. Peel the carrots and thinly slice diagonally. Thinly slice the scallions. Set aside. In a small bowl, blend the soy sauce, honey, and sesame oil. Set aside.

2. Heat a large heavy skillet or wok over high heat. Add 1 tablespoon of the oil. Add the cashews and stir-fry until lightly browned, 45 seconds. Transfer the cashews to a medium bowl.

3. Add the turkey and stir-fry until lightly golden, 2 to 3 minutes. Transfer the turkey to the bowl with the cashews and set aside.

4. Warm the remaining 1 tablespoon of oil in the skillet over medium-high heat. Add the carrots and scallions and stir-fry until crisp-tender, about 2 minutes. Add the asparagus and stir-fry for 2 minutes.

5. Stir the soy sauce mixture and add it to the skillet. Return the turkey and cashews to the skillet and stir-fry just until heated through, 2 to 3 minutes. Serve hot.

Turkey Scallopini

 ♡ LOW-FAT

⅓ CUP FLOUR
½ TEASPOON DRIED SAGE
¼ TEASPOON SALT
⅛ TEASPOON BLACK PEPPER
4 TURKEY BREAST CUTLETS (ABOUT
   1 POUND TOTAL), POUNDED ¼
   INCH THICK

1 TABLESPOON UNSALTED BUTTER
1 TABLESPOON VEGETABLE OIL
3 TABLESPOONS BALSAMIC VINEGAR
ONE 16-OUNCE CAN WHOLE
   TOMATOES, DRAINED AND CHOPPED

1. On a sheet of wax paper, combine the flour, ¼ teaspoon of the sage, the salt, and pepper. Dredge the turkey cutlets in the flour mixture, shaking off the excess.

2. In a large skillet, warm the butter and oil over medium-high heat. Add the turkey cutlets and cook until browned and cooked through, 2 to 3 minutes per side. Transfer the turkey to a serving platter and cover loosely with foil to keep warm.

3. Pour the vinegar into the skillet, stirring to scrape up any browned bits. Boil for 30 seconds. Stir in the tomatoes and the remaining ¼ teaspoon of the sage. Cook over medium heat, stirring frequently, for 2 minutes.

4. Spoon the sauce over the turkey cutlets and serve hot.

TURKEY SLOPPY JOES

SERVES 4

♡ LOW-FAT

1 TABLESPOON VEGETABLE OIL
1 POUND GROUND TURKEY
1 LARGE ONION, CHOPPED
2 GARLIC CLOVES, MINCED
2 TEASPOONS CHILI POWDER
ONE 8-OUNCE CAN TOMATO SAUCE

½ CUP BEEF BROTH, PREFERABLY
  REDUCED-SODIUM
1 TABLESPOON WORCESTERSHIRE
  SAUCE
¼ TEASPOON SALT
⅛ TEASPOON BLACK PEPPER
4 ONION ROLLS, SPLIT

1. In a large skillet, warm the oil over medium-high heat. Add the turkey, breaking up the meat with a large spoon, and cook until browned, stirring frequently, about 5 minutes.

2. Reduce the heat to medium and stir in the onion and garlic. Cook until the onion is softened, 3 to 4 minutes. Stir in the chili powder and cook for 1 minute.

3. Add the tomato sauce, beef broth, and Worcestershire sauce. Cook, stirring occasionally, until thickened, about 5 minutes. Season with the salt and pepper.

4. Meanwhile, toast the rolls. Spoon the mixture over the bottom halves of the rolls, replace the tops, and serve.

Turkey Fajitas

SERVES 4

♡ LOW-FAT

EIGHT 7-INCH FLOUR TORTILLAS
2 TEASPOONS CHILI POWDER
½ TEASPOON GROUND CUMIN
½ TEASPOON DRIED OREGANO
12 OUNCES TURKEY BREAST CUTLETS
2 TEASPOONS VEGETABLE OIL
1 MEDIUM ONION, HALVED AND
    THINLY SLICED

1 MEDIUM GREEN BELL PEPPER, HALVED
    AND THINLY SLICED
1 MEDIUM RED BELL PEPPER, HALVED
    AND THINLY SLICED
2 CUPS SHREDDED ICEBERG LETTUCE
½ CUP BOTTLED SALSA

1. Preheat the oven to 225°. Wrap the tortillas in foil and place in the oven to warm while making the fajita filling.

2. On a sheet of wax paper, combine the chili powder, cumin, and oregano. Rub the spice mixture onto both sides of the turkey cutlets.

3. In a large nonstick skillet, warm 1 teaspoon of the oil over medium-high heat. Add the onion and bell peppers and sauté until lightly browned and crisp-tender, about 3 minutes. Transfer the vegetables to a bowl and cover with foil to keep warm.

4. Warm the remaining 1 teaspoon of oil in the skillet over medium-high heat. Add the turkey cutlets and cook until browned and just cooked through, 2 to 3 minutes per side. Transfer the turkey cutlets to a cutting board and slice crosswise into narrow strips.

5. Top each warm tortilla with some shredded lettuce and a spoonful of salsa. Arrange the sliced turkey and vegetables down the center. Fold the tortillas around the filling and arrange on a serving platter.

JAMBALAYA

SERVES 4

1 TABLESPOON VEGETABLE OIL
½ POUND FULLY COOKED SMOKED
SAUSAGE, SUCH AS ANDOUILLE OR
KIELBASA, SLICED ¼ INCH THICK
1 MEDIUM ONION, CHOPPED
1 LARGE GREEN BELL PEPPER, CHOPPED
1 GARLIC CLOVE, MINCED
1 TEASPOON DRIED THYME

½ TEASPOON TURMERIC
1 CUP RICE
ONE 14½-OUNCE CAN STEWED
TOMATOES
1 CUP CHICKEN BROTH, PREFERABLY
REDUCED-SODIUM
½ POUND COOKED, PEELED MEDIUM
SHRIMP

1. In a large skillet, warm the oil over medium-high heat. Add the sausage and sauté until browned, about 4 minutes. Transfer the sausage to a plate.

2. Add the onion and bell pepper and sauté until softened, about 3 minutes. Add the garlic, thyme, turmeric, and rice, and cook, stirring, for 30 seconds.

3. Return the sausage to the skillet and add the tomatoes and chicken broth. Bring the mixture to a boil. Reduce the heat to medium, cover, and simmer until the rice is tender and the liquid is absorbed, about 15 minutes.

4. Stir in the shrimp and cook, stirring occasionally, just until heated through, about 2 minutes.

SWEET AFTERTHOUGHT: *A Louisiana-style dinner such as jambalaya calls for an equally Southern dessert. Try this version of Bananas Foster: In a large skillet, melt 4 tablespoons unsalted butter and add ¼ cup brown sugar and a pinch of ground cinnamon and nutmeg. Peel and slice 4 medium bananas lengthwise. Add them to the skillet and sauté until they begin to brown, about 1 minute per side. Place 2 banana halves on each plate, top with a scoop of vanilla ice cream, and pour over any remaining sauce.*

Maryland Crab Cakes

SERVES 4

TWO 6½-OUNCE CANS CRABMEAT, DRAINED WELL

¼ CUP UNSEASONED DRY BREAD CRUMBS

2 TABLESPOONS REDUCED-FAT MAYONNAISE

1 LARGE EGG

1 TEASPOON OLD BAY SEASONING

¼ CUP FLOUR

¼ TEASPOON SALT

¼ TEASPOON BLACK PEPPER

2 TABLESPOONS VEGETABLE OIL

½ CUP BOTTLED TARTAR SAUCE (OPTIONAL)

LEMON WEDGES (OPTIONAL)

1. In a medium bowl, mix the crabmeat, bread crumbs, mayonnaise, egg, and seasoning until blended. Form the mixture into eight 3-inch patties.

2. On a sheet of wax paper, combine the flour, salt, and pepper. Dredge the patties in the flour mixture, shaking off the excess.

3. In a large skillet, warm the oil over medium heat. Add the crab cakes and cook in batches as necessary until browned and cooked through, 2 to 3 minutes per side. Transfer the crab cakes to paper towels to drain.

4. Serve the crab cakes with tartar sauce and lemon wedges, if desired.

KITCHEN NOTE: *If you do not have tartar sauce on hand you can easily mix some up by combining ½ cup of mayonnaise, ¼ cup of sweet pickle relish, 1 teaspoon Dijon mustard, and 2 tablespoons vegetable oil.*

Honey-Glazed Shrimp

SERVES 4

3 TABLESPOONS UNSALTED BUTTER
¼ CUP FINELY CHOPPED ONION
1 GARLIC CLOVE, MINCED
½ TEASPOON TURMERIC
½ TEASPOON CARDAMOM
½ TEASPOON CINNAMON

⅛ TEASPOON CAYENNE PEPPER
1 TABLESPOON GRATED LEMON ZEST
¼ CUP FRESH LEMON JUICE
2 POUNDS UNCOOKED LARGE SHRIMP,
  SHELLED WITH TAILS LEFT ON
1½ TABLESPOONS HONEY

1. In a large skillet, warm the butter over medium heat until melted. Add the onion and garlic and sauté until the onion is softened, about 3 minutes.

2. Stir in the turmeric, cardamom, cinnamon, cayenne, lemon zest, and lemon juice, and cook for 1 minute.

3. Add the shrimp and cook over medium-high heat, stirring frequently, until pink.

4. Add the honey and cook, stirring frequently, until the honey is melted and the shrimps are coated. Serve hot.

Snapper with Tomato-Olive Sauce

SERVES 4

⅓ CUP FLOUR

½ TEASPOON SALT

¼ TEASPOON BLACK PEPPER

1½ POUNDS RED SNAPPER FILLETS

3 TABLESPOONS UNSALTED BUTTER

1 GARLIC CLOVE, MINCED

6 PLUM TOMATOES, COARSELY CHOPPED

2 TABLESPOONS BALSAMIC VINEGAR

¾ CUP CHICKEN BROTH, PREFERABLY REDUCED-SODIUM

⅓ CUP CHOPPED BLACK OLIVES

1. On a sheet of wax paper, combine the flour, salt, and pepper. Dredge each side of the fillets in the flour mixture, shaking off the excess.

2. In a medium skillet, warm 2 tablespoons of the butter over medium-high heat until melted. Add the fish, skin side up, and cook until just done, about 5 minutes. Turn the fish and cook on the skin side for 1 minute. Transfer the fish fillets to warm serving plates.

3. Add the garlic, tomatoes, vinegar, and chicken broth to the skillet. Bring to a boil over medium-high heat and simmer until the liquid is reduced to ½ cup, about 3 minutes.

4. Remove the pan from the heat and stir in the olives and remaining 1 tablespoon of butter. Spoon the sauce over the fish and serve right away.

Substitution: *Salmon fillets are also delicious when they are served with this tomato-olive sauce.*

Curried Scallop Sauté

SERVES 4

♡ LOW - FAT

2 TEASPOONS VEGETABLE OIL

2 MEDIUM CARROTS, PEELED AND CUT
   INTO THIN STRIPS

1 MEDIUM CELERY RIB, CUT INTO THIN
   STRIPS

¾ CUP WHITE WINE

1 TEASPOON MINCED GARLIC

1 TEASPOON DIJON MUSTARD

1 TEASPOON CORNSTARCH

½ TEASPOON CURRY POWDER

½ TEASPOON HONEY

1 POUND FRESH SEA SCALLOPS

¼ TEASPOON SALT

¼ TEASPOON BLACK PEPPER

1. In a large nonstick skillet, heat 1 teaspoon of the oil over medium-high heat. Add the carrots and celery and sauté until softened, about 10 minutes. Transfer the vegetables to a serving platter and cover loosely with foil to keep warm.

2. Meanwhile, in a glass measuring cup, blend the wine, garlic, mustard, cornstarch, curry powder, and honey.

3. Warm the remaining teaspoon of oil in the skillet over medium-high heat. Add the scallops and sauté for 1 minute.

4. Stir the wine mixture and add it to the skillet. Cook, stirring frequently, until the scallops are opaque throughout and the sauce has thickened slightly, 2 to 3 minutes. Stir in the salt and pepper. Spoon the scallops and sauce over the vegetables and serve.

Mixed Greens with Mustard Vinaigrette

SERVES 4

6 CUPS LIGHTLY PACKED TORN
  LETTUCE, SUCH AS ROMAINE, GREEN
  OR RED LEAF, OR A COMBINATION
2 CUPS LIGHTLY PACKED TORN BITTER
  GREENS, SUCH AS CHICORY,
  RADICCHIO, OR BELGIAN ENDIVE
2 TABLESPOONS RED WINE VINEGAR

½ TEASPOON MINCED GARLIC
  (OPTIONAL)
1 TEASPOON DIJON MUSTARD
¼ CUP OLIVE OIL
¼ CUP VEGETABLE OIL
SALT AND BLACK PEPPER TO TASTE

1. Rinse the lettuce and greens and spin dry. Toss together in a large serving bowl.

2. In a small bowl, whisk together the vinegar, garlic, if desired, and the mustard. Slowly whisk in the oil until blended. Season with salt and pepper.

3. Just before serving, whisk the dressing again and pour over the greens. Toss to mix and coat evenly.

Variation: *This simple green salad is perfect on its own, but it is also extremely versatile when mixed with other ingredients. Try adding fruits and nuts for an interesting blend of color, texture, and flavor. Thinly slice 2 ripe pears, arrange them over the top of the salad, and sprinkle with ⅓ cup toasted chopped walnuts. Or toss the salad with 2 diced apples, 1 cup diced Cheddar cheese, and the walnuts.*

Romaine Hearts with Creamy Parmesan Dressing and Bacon

SERVES 4

3 SLICES BACON

8 CUPS LIGHTLY PACKED TORN
ROMAINE HEARTS

¼ CUP MAYONNAISE

2 TABLESPOONS RED WINE VINEGAR

2 TABLESPOONS GRATED PARMESAN
CHEESE

1 TABLESPOON DIJON MUSTARD

1 TABLESPOON CHOPPED FRESH BASIL,
OR 1 TEASPOON DRIED

⅛ TEASPOON SALT

1. Cook the bacon in a medium skillet over medium heat until crisp, about 7 minutes. Transfer the bacon to paper towels to drain.

2. Wash the Romaine and spin dry.

3. In a small bowl, mix the mayonnaise, vinegar, Parmesan cheese, mustard, basil, and salt until well blended.

4. Put the Romaine in a large serving bowl. Spoon over the dressing and toss to coat. Crumble the bacon and sprinkle over the top.

KITCHEN NOTE: *Romaine hearts are the inner leaves from heads of Romaine lettuce. They are crisper and less bitter than the outer leaves and are often sold packaged near the prepackaged salad greens. If they are unavailable, you can use one large head of Romaine lettuce.*

Citrus Salad with Leafy Greens

SERVES 4

6 CUPS LIGHTLY PACKED TORN RED OR
  GREEN LEAF LETTUCE
2 CUPS LIGHTLY PACKED WATERCRESS,
  COARSE STEMS REMOVED
2 TABLESPOONS FRESH ORANGE JUICE
1 TABLESPOON WHITE WINE VINEGAR

½ TEASPOON GRATED ORANGE ZEST
½ TEASPOON POPPY SEEDS
¼ CUP VEGETABLE OIL
⅛ TEASPOON SALT
2 MEDIUM NAVEL ORANGES
1 LARGE PINK GRAPEFRUIT

1. Rinse the lettuce and watercress and spin dry. Toss together in a large serving bowl.

2. In a small bowl, whisk together the orange juice, vinegar, orange zest, and poppy seeds. Slowly whisk in the oil until blended. Season with the salt.

3. Using a sharp knife, remove the peel and white pith from the oranges and grapefruit, slicing a piece off the top and bottom. Slice the oranges into rounds and cut the grapefruit in half lengthwise, then slice crosswise. Remove all the seeds.

4. Whisk the vinaigrette, pour half over the greens, and toss well to coat evenly. Divide the greens among 4 serving plates and arrange the fruit on top, alternating the slices. Drizzle with the remaining vinaigrette.

Garlic-Mozzarella Bread

SERVES 6 TO 8

4 TABLESPOONS UNSALTED BUTTER, AT
  ROOM TEMPERATURE
¼ CUP CHOPPED FRESH PARSLEY
2 GARLIC CLOVES, FORCED THROUGH A
  PRESS
¼ TEASPOON BLACK PEPPER
1 LOAF CRUSTY ITALIAN OR FRENCH
  BREAD (ABOUT 12 INCHES IN
  LENGTH)
½ CUP SHREDDED MOZZARELLA CHEESE

1. In a small bowl, blend the butter, parsley, garlic, and pepper.

2. Preheat the broiler. Slice the bread in half lengthwise and spread the butter mixture over the cut sides, leaving a ¼-inch border all around. Sprinkle each half with the cheese.

3. Broil the bread 6 inches from the heat until the cheese is melted and the edges are crisp and brown, 2 to 3 minutes. Cut into slices and serve right away.

VARIATION: *To give this bread a completely different flavor, omit the mozzarella cheese and add ½ cup crumbled Gorgonzola cheese to the butter mixture. Spread the mixture over the bread and broil as directed.*

GRILLED TOMATO-BASIL TOASTS

SERVES 4

One-half loaf crusty Italian or
　French bread (about 12 inches
　in length)
1 tablespoon reduced-fat
　mayonnaise
1 tablespoon olive oil

1 tablespoon tomato paste
2 tablespoons chopped fresh basil,
　or 2 teaspoons dried
1 garlic clove, minced
⅛ teaspoon salt
⅛ teaspoon pepper

1. Preheat the broiler or prepare the grill. Cut the bread in half lengthwise, then cut each piece in half.

2. In a small bowl, blend the mayonnaise, olive oil, tomato paste, basil, garlic, salt, and pepper.

3. Grill or broil the bread, cut sides 4 inches from the heat, until lightly toasted, 1 to 2 minutes. Spread the tomato-garlic mixture over each piece and serve warm.

Kitchen Note: *These toasts can be spread with almost anything including your favorite purchased dip or spread. Serve them with soup, stews, pasta dishes, or main-dish salads.*

FAVORITE FRIED RICE

SERVES 6

♡ LOW-FAT

2 CUPS PLUS 1 TABLESPOON REDUCED-
  SODIUM CHICKEN BROTH OR WATER
1 CUP RICE
1 TABLESPOON PLUS 1 TEASPOON
  PEANUT OIL
3 LARGE EGGS
⅛ TEASPOON SALT
2 TABLESPOONS OYSTER SAUCE

1 TABLESPOON SOY SAUCE
½ TEASPOON ORIENTAL (DARK) SESAME
  OIL
1½ TEASPOONS MINCED FRESH GINGER
1 CUP FROZEN GREEN PEAS, THAWED
1 CUP FROZEN CORN KERNELS, THAWED
4 SCALLIONS, THINLY SLICED

1. In a medium saucepan, bring 2 cups of the chicken broth to a boil over high heat. Add the rice. Cover, reduce the heat to medium-low, and simmer for 15 minutes. Remove the pan from the heat and let stand for 5 minutes, until the rice is tender and the liquid is absorbed.

2. Meanwhile, in a large skillet, warm 1 tablespoon of the oil over medium-high heat. Lightly beat the eggs with the salt. Pour the eggs into the skillet and cook, stirring with a fork, until scrambled, 2 to 3 minutes. Transfer to a plate and break up into small pieces.

3. In a small bowl, combine the remaining tablespoon of chicken broth, the oyster sauce, soy sauce, and sesame oil.

4. Warm the remaining teaspoon of oil in the skillet over medium-high heat. Add the ginger and stir-fry for 10 seconds. Add the peas and corn and stir-fry for 20 seconds. Add the cooked rice and stir-fry until heated through, 2 to 3 minutes.

5. Add the oyster sauce mixture to the skillet and stir until the rice is thoroughly coated. Stir in the eggs and scallions and serve.

⊙RZO VERDE

SERVES 6

1¼ CUPS ORZO
ONE 10-OUNCE PACKAGE FROZEN
    CHOPPED BROCCOLI
2 TABLESPOONS OLIVE OIL

¼ TEASPOON SALT
¼ TEASPOON BLACK PEPPER
¼ CUP GRATED PARMESAN CHEESE

1. Cook the orzo in a medium pot of boiling water until al dente according to the package directions.

2. Meanwhile, cook the broccoli according to the package directions.

3. Drain the orzo. Drain the broccoli and press out excess liquid.

4. In a medium bowl, combine the orzo, broccoli, olive oil, salt, and pepper. Add the Parmesan cheese and toss well to mix.

KITCHEN NOTE: *Although orzo means barley in Italian, it is actually a small rice-shaped pasta. This quick and colorful side dish makes a wonderful accompaniment to steaks, pork chops, or chicken. It can also be made using chopped frozen spinach in place of the broccoli to provide the color "verde."*

HERBED RICE PILAF

SERVES 4

♡ LOW-FAT

2 TABLESPOONS BUTTER
1 MEDIUM ONION, FINELY CHOPPED
1 CUP RICE
½ TEASPOON DRIED BASIL

½ TEASPOON DRIED THYME
¼ TEASPOON SALT
¼ TEASPOON BLACK PEPPER

1. In a medium saucepan, melt the butter over medium heat. Add the onion and cook, stirring frequently, until softened, about 5 minutes. Add the rice, basil, thyme, salt, and pepper, and cook, stirring constantly, for 1 minute.

2. Add 2 cups water and bring to a boil over medium-high heat. Cover, reduce the heat to low, and simmer for 20 minutes, until the rice is tender and the liquid is absorbed.

KITCHEN NOTE: *No peeking! Lifting the lid to peek at rice while it's cooking lets the steam out and slows down the cooking process. Also, the lid should be tight-fitting to prevent steam from escaping. If yours is loose, cover the pan with a sheet of wax paper, punch a hole in the center, then place the lid over it.*

Black Bean Salsa

SERVES 4 TO 6

One 15-ounce can black beans,
    rinsed and drained
One 11-ounce can vacuum-packed
    corn kernels
2 medium tomatoes, diced
1 small red bell pepper, diced
1 small green bell pepper, diced
¼ cup finely chopped red onion

1 to 2 jalapeño peppers, seeded
    and finely chopped
⅓ cup fresh lime juice
⅓ cup olive oil
¼ cup chopped fresh cilantro
½ teaspoon ground cumin
½ teaspoon salt

1. In a large bowl, combine the beans, corn, tomatoes, bell peppers, onion, and jalapeño.

2. Add the lime juice, olive oil, cilantro, cumin, and salt, and toss well to combine and coat evenly.

Kitchen Note: *Capsaicin, the substance contained in the interior ribs of hot peppers, can cause a burning sensation on your skin. Wear rubber gloves when peeling, seeding, and slicing them, and remember not to rub your eyes, mouth, or sensitive areas around your nose.*

WILD MUSHROOM STIR-FRY

SERVES 4

2 SLICES BACON, CUT INTO 1-INCH
PIECES
1 GARLIC CLOVE, MINCED
½ POUND MIXED FRESH WILD
MUSHROOMS (SUCH AS SHIITAKE,
CHANTERELLES, AND OYSTER),
STEMMED AND QUARTERED

2 TABLESPOONS CHOPPED FRESH
PARSLEY
½ TEASPOON SALT
¼ TEASPOON BLACK PEPPER

1. Cook the bacon in a large skillet or wok over medium-high heat until crisp, about 6 minutes. Transfer the bacon to paper towels to drain. Set aside.

2. Pour off all but 2 tablespoons of the drippings. Add the garlic and stir-fry for 20 seconds; do not let the garlic burn. Add the mushrooms and stir-fry until tender and softened, 3 to 4 minutes.

3. Stir in the parsley, salt, pepper, and reserved bacon. Serve right away.

KITCHEN NOTE: *Store fresh mushrooms, unwashed, in the refrigerator for up to 3 days. Mushrooms are extremely absorbent and will soak up any moisture available, which will cause them to decay rapidly. To avoid this, store mushrooms wrapped in paper towels or a kitchen towel. This will allow air to circulate and provide a surface to absorb any moisture.*

Sautéed Spinach with Garlic

SERVES 4

3 TABLESPOONS OLIVE OIL

2 GARLIC CLOVES, CRUSHED WITH THE
SIDE OF A KNIFE

2 POUNDS FRESH SPINACH, STEMMED
AND WELL RINSED

¼ TEASPOON SALT

⅛ TEASPOON BLACK PEPPER

1. In a saucepan large enough to hold all the spinach, warm the oil over medium heat. Add the garlic and sauté for 1 minute.

2. Add the spinach and stir quickly and constantly with the garlic until spinach is wilted, 3 to

4 minutes. Season with salt and pepper, and cook for 1 to 2 minutes until spinach is tender but not overcooked.

3. Discard the garlic and serve.

KITCHEN NOTE: *Place the unpeeled garlic cloves between the flat side of a chef's knife and a cutting board and press firmly on the knife with the heel of your hand to crush them. This method separates the skin for easy removal.*

CREAMY POTATO SALAD

1¼ POUNDS SMALL UNPEELED RED POTATOES (1 TO 1½ INCHES IN DIAMETER), CUT IN HALF OR QUARTERED DEPENDING ON THEIR SIZE

½ CUP REDUCED-FAT MAYONNAISE

2 TABLESPOONS BUTTERMILK

1 TEASPOON DIJON MUSTARD

½ CUP THINLY SLICED CELERY

2 TABLESPOONS CHOPPED FRESH PARSLEY

¼ TEASPOON SALT

¼ TEASPOON BLACK PEPPER

1 TABLESPOON CHOPPED FRESH CHIVES OR SCALLION GREENS

1. Place the potatoes in a steamer set over 1 inch of boiling water. Cover and steam until just tender, about 12 minutes.

2. Meanwhile, in a small bowl, combine the mayonnaise, buttermilk, and mustard.

3. Transfer the potatoes to a serving bowl. Add the celery, parsley, salt, and pepper, and toss gently to combine. Let stand for 10 minutes to cool the potatoes.

4. Stir the mayonnaise mixture, pour it over the salad, and toss well to coat evenly. Sprinkle with the chives and serve.

İnDEX